## About the Author

Joe Remesz was born in Bonnyville, Alberta and graduated from Lorne Greene's Academy Radio and Television Arts in Toronto and began his career as a copy writer in that city. Later he worked as a radio announcer in United States and Canada and as a news director with station CJAT in Trail B. C. In 1978 Joe retired from broadcasting and moved to Penticton, B. C. where he became a real estate salesman with Block Brothers,

Joe has traveled extensively throughout the world and now totally retired lives in Edmonton and Southern Leyte, Philippines. At age 83 he writes novels, short stories and limericks. Joe is an avid fan of the Edmonton Oilers/Eskimos and Toronto Blue Jays.

# CHAPTER ONE

There have been three Ukrainian immigrations to Canada, each differing in numbers, the conditions in Canada which attracted them and the conditions in their homeland which made them leave. The first and largest immigration began in 1891 and with the coming of the First World War, the second immigration arrived between the two wars, the third began in 1946 and is still continuing although the numbers have been reduced to a trickle.

The number of people arriving is estimated to be about 170,000 for the first immigration, about 68,000 for the second and about 37,000 for the third.

Although eighty percent of the Ukraine's land was part of the Russian empire, most landed on Canadian shores during this period were from the western portion, then under Austrian rule. The first immigration consisted most entirely of land-hungry peasants from the provinces of Galecia and Bukovina.

Denied any opportunity to improve their lot in their homeland, they were attracted to Canada by its policy granted by the Liberal Wilfred Laurier government to colonize Western Canada by offering one-hundred and sixty acres of land for the sum of ten dollars to the settlers.

Wasyl Elaniak, Ivan Philipiw and Dr. Josef Oleskiw are commonly considered to be the first leading Ukrainian immigrants in Western prairie Canada that used their influence to attract other Ukrainians to come as families and settled in colonies in the localities of Edna, Bruderheim, Chipman, Lamont, Smokey Lake and Vegreville, near Edmonton and Winnipeg and other parts of Manitoba and Saskatchewan.

The second immigration (1922-1939) was smaller than the first and after the Ukrainian Republic had fallen and the partion between Poland, Romania, Czech-Slovakia and Russia was completed. And the danger of another war began plus coming of the Great Depression not all were able to make adjustments to the new condition encountering protests by both the Canadian English and French speaking.

Still in some ways the two immigrations contributed to the Canadian population and economy and the Ukrainian immigrants are proud to be Canadians and Canada is proud to have them.

Bonnyville was established as a village September 19, 1929 with Dr. Severin Sabourin as mayor. Prior to this date the community was known as St. Louis de Moose Lake. Bonnyville was incorporated as a town February 16, 1948 with Alfred Muller as the first mayor.

It was early in 1907 that Father Therien saw the first evidence of success in colonizing this part in the province of Alberta. He had gone to visit a friend in Beaumont, a small French Canadian settlement fifteen miles south of Edmonton. There he succeeded in challenging Philorome Oullette, age twenty-five, Wilfred Ouimet age forty-five, Albert Dargis, age twenty-one to venture into the Moose Lake area. Twenty-four year old Honorius Lamareau joined later.

Towards the end of 1907 the first eight pioneers arrived: Wilfred Ouimet, Albert Dargis, Philorome Outlette plus Aime Marcotte, Hormidas Boisvert, Joseph Mercier, Oliva Martel and Come Ouimet. The rest is history. They found the land thickly wooded and dotted with lakes and sloughs. Frequently these sloughs were fringed with meadows on which cattle could be pastured and from which succulent hay could be harvested. Much of the land around the lakes was rocky, but in general among innumerable trees and under the fallen tree trunks layer of leaves; they found a thick layer of fertile black soil. Surveying of parcels of land had not been completed yet. Some pioneers used oxen as draught animals because they had no horses.

In 1908, the first school was established in the hamlet of Bonnyville by Ernestine Ouimet to teach seven students while Father Bonny (Catholic) and Reverend John Duclos (Presbyterian) built the first churches.
And in 1915, as a result of a petition circulated by Pierre Robitaille, the municipal district of Bonnyville was formed.

During that time, a young pilot named Grant McConachie flew fresh fish from the surrounding lakes, including Cold Lake, to a train where it was shipped to Chicago and New York. His business continued to expand until it became Canadian Airways. The Canadian National Railway built a line that reached Bonnyville in 1928 and on the September 2, the following year, Bonnyville was established as a village. Twenty years later it became a town.

Like most of the Canadian West, Bonnyville has its historical roots entwined in the fur traders, Indians and missionaries. The first European to arrive in the land of the Cree and Chipewyan was a Scotsman named Angus Shaw, a fur trader for the North West Company. During his life Shaw also worked as a politician, military officer and Justice of the Peace before ending up on the wrong side of the law.

Shaw first came to North Central Alberta in 1789 to trade fur for the North West Company and that year established the first European settlement called Anshaw, just west of

Bonnyville and a fur trade post at Moose Lake at the time called Lac de L'Original.

Shaw led a respectable life. He was admitted to various clubs including the Beaver Club and the Canada Club in London. He also spent two years in Federal politic serving as a member of the Rffingham in the House of Assembly in the Lower House from 1802 to 1804. Shaw also acted as Justice of the Peace for the Indian Territory from 1810 to 1816. During the war of 1812 between Canada and United States Shaw participated in the capture of Michilimackinac (Mackimac Island, Michigan) from the Americans and on October 3, was appointed a major in the Corps of Canadian Voyagers.

The fur trade was in Shaw's blood and 'Le Chat' as he was nicknamed, took on an active part in the final phase of the struggle between the North West and Hudson Bay Company. During 1885 Shaw was at Red River, Manitoba, where he tried to break up the colony and for that reason in March 1816 Lord Douglas Selkirk had him arrested. Two years later Shaw was arrested again at Grand

Rapids, Manitoba by the Hudson Bay
Company governor William Williams.

Because Shaw threatened to come back and
spread bloodshed and terror throughout the
country once released, Williams decided to
keep Shaw as a prisoner,
 Shaw was transferred to the York factory and
from there to London where he was set free.
After the amalgamation of the two companies
in 1821 Shaw retired to the United States,
where he was out of reach of lawsuits arising
from some questionable business dealings.

Shaw died in United States in 1832 of a
pulmonary disorder a wealthy man. He had
shares in the Bank of Montreal and the
Hudson Bay Company and owned properties
on both sides of the border.

When Shaw was getting into trouble in
eastern Canada, a more peaceful process was
taking place back in Bonnyville.
The turn of the century saw three waves of
Europeans settle in the area between the years
1907 and 1918. Among the first were French
Catholic missionaries, including Oblate

priests. In the autumn of 1906 Charles Lirette left Lowell. Massachusetts to explore the Moose Lake region where game was plentiful that he built a trappers cabin on the big island of Moose Lake and another on the bank of Beaver River at a spot called Rat Lake, approximately sixteen miles northeast of the present site of Bonnyville. During the 1906-07 winter Lirette established a trap line ranging from a cabin on the Beaver River, all the way to Winfred Lake, approximately eighty-five miles north of Bonnyville. At the time the area was teeming with beavers and muskrats.

And then Reverend Father Francois Bonny (1908 -1910) after whom Bonnyville takes its name, and Father Adeodat Therien, who was encouraged by Father Albert Lacombe to help the Metis (of mixed Native/European heritage) settle in Northeastern Alberta appeared on the scene. The town of Therien near Bonnyville bears his name.

At the time of this writing Bonnyville, a three hour drive northeast of Edmonton, has a population of approximately 7,000 and its economy is based on nearby oil reserves and agricultural resources and the home to numerous French-speaking and Ukrainian Canadians.

And thirteen miles south of the town is the Kehewin Cree First Nation Reseeve. A bit further is a Metis settlement.

A large crowd came to watch a passenger train arrive at the Bonnyville CNR station. The brilliant sun had already exploded into shimmering multi-colors and was about to set on a warm August 1928 evening. Another wave of east and central European immigrants had begun to Alberta

Originally fur traders had planted seeds of colonization in Western Canada but since then, the job had been done by individual agencies: railway builders, gold prospectors, missionaries, revolutionaries and homesteaders. While those of Ukrainian heritage had already settled near Edmonton it wasn't until the Canadian National Railway link was completed from the capital of Alberta that they began settling around Bonnyville in east central part of Alberta.

Ukrainian pioneers helped tame the forests and the prairies by contending not only with a hostile environment, but also, like in Manitoba and especially in Winnipeg earlier, with a social environment contentious towards the immigrants from east and central Europe. Ukrainian and Polish immigrants were part of a wave of peasants from Galicia, Bukovina and Transcarpathia of the Austria-Hungarian Empire until the end of World War 1. They were often described in early immigration records as Austrians, Galician's, Bukowinians, Rutherians, Little Russians, Routhanians, and Galatians.

The first immigration the duel religious base upon which their identity was to grow. Those from Galicia were Greek Catholic, those from Bukovina were Greek Orthodox, and this division still prevails their lives today.

.

It began in the 1890's after trailblazers: Ivan Pylpow, Wasyl Elaniak and Dr. Josef Oleskiw encouraged their friends, against the wishes of their government, to move to Canada where one could have land that is free and be his own master.

This particular train had not only Ukrainian immigrants on board, but also a bearded Jewish bachelor, Abraham Goldman, who operated the Goldman General Store in Bonnyville, and Lee Wong who operated the Royal Chinese Restaurant.

Other passengers that disembarked among a polyglot of tongues, included Jacques and Yvette Gateau and their children: Marcel, ten, and Gloria, eleven. The Gateau's were recent arrivals from the province of Quebec, but receiving more attention than anyone else were Europeans who couldn't speak English or French and termed as Bohemians, in this case Ukrainians, and Poles, who disembarked and came through the station: the whiskered men in sheepskin coats, the tired women with bundles, the frightened children, each of the Ukrainians came with a handful of earth wrapped in a handkerchiefs, to be thrown into his or her grave once they had died. This included Evdokia Kowalchuk, and her two children, Kwitka, nine and Pawel, eleven. They were the last to get off the train. The Kowalchuk's were used to being last because they were Ukrainian.

The Kowalchuk family was also encouraged to come to Canada by Pawlo Bilyi and Petro Czorny who as immigrants, arrived in Winnipeg prior to World War 1 and eventually established a thriving business called Mancan which distributed Ukrainian food throughout Manitoba.

But before this happened, they had to Anglicize their Slav name from Pawlo Bily to Paul White and Petro Czorny to Peter Black.

Roman, Evdokia's husband, came to Canada a year before his wife and wasn't able to welcome his family to Canada. Nick and Olga Barba, who at one time lived in the same village near Lvov as the Kowalchuk's, welcomed them instead. Roman was still in the local RCMP lockup serving a three-day sentence for losing his temper and then assaulting a French-speaking store clerk who called Roman, "The scum of Europe."

But even the Barba's were surprised when at the last minute Roman was let out of the lockup and embraced his wife and children. It was as if an answer to a prayer that Roman walked up to his wife and while embracing her say, "Evdokia, welcome to Canada. It's nice to see you again."

"And it's nice to be with you again," Evdokia replied.

With Roman was a heavy set bald headed man of German heritage whose parents had no religious affiliation but William Aberhart Jr., later in life became a Christian, first a Presbyterian and then a Baptist. He was wearing small glasses not attached to his ears when he visited Roman at the lockup and convinced an Anglo RCMP Sergeant, David Livingston that Roman posed no danger to society and should be set free so that he could meet his family.

The man who helped Roman identified himself as William Aberhart also known as 'Bible Bill' for his outspoken Baptist views. During the conversation that followed Bible Bill said he was a teacher and a leader of a fundamentalist religious organization called *The Prophetic Bible Institute* in Calgary. Aberhart already had a religious program on radio station *CFCN* in Calgary called *Back to the Bible* and in his sermons believed the reason for the depression was that people did not have enough money to spend so the government should give everyone $25 a month to stimulate the economy and he was in Bonnyville as he phrased it: "To help the poor farmers in Alberta and then in Saskatchewan." When followers of his faith told Aberhart about Roman's predicament he said to them, "I'll see what I can do to have Mr. Kowalchuk released."

And he did.

When Roman first met Aberhart at the police station, Roman felt Aberhart was a highly respected preacher who helped the poor but did not understand what Aberhart meant when he often said," It's the rooster that makes the noise but the hen lays the eggs."

Bonnyville, population 1000, was predominantly a tight-knit French community although a concentration of Europeans was beginning to arrive to seek a better life for themselves and their children. Roman however, could not help overhearing snide remarks as he hugged his wife and children. Remarks like: "The Bohunks smell garlic." And, "Look at those Hunkies in their sheepskin coats and babushkas."

Evdokia had a comment too, on Roman's appearance, after Aberhart introduced himself to the Kowalchuk family and had left. Evdokia noticed Roman's sunburned face and said to him, "Now that we have arrived in the Promised Land, where do we go from here?" "We are going to drive to Nick and Olga's Barba's farm where they will put us up until we are able to move into our own home that I'm building."

Roman was proud of the single room house he was building on his quarter section of land that was situated adjacent to Barba's and across the road from a homestead recently claimed by Jacques Gateau and his family. "Our home is near three lakes: Jessie, Moose and Muriel. There's an unnamed creek running through the property where one catches a fish with a bare hand plus many trees:

Poplar, spruce, birch and tamarack that can be used for fire wood and there are a different variety of birds. For ten-dollars it's a bargain, believe me." Roman assured Evdokia describing the 160 acre homestead he had

claimed from the Land Office for ten-dollars.
"And I'm not finished.

"Besides the chokecherry, pin- cherry,
saskatoon and other wild berries, there are
wild roses and other flowers whose names I
do not know, everywhere. The air is so sweet
with their perfume that when bumblebees,
humming birds and butterflies land on them,
the birds, bees and butterflies seem
energized."

Roman and Evdokia embraced another time
and then when a trunk filled with clothing and
memorabilia from Ukraine, was placed into a
wagon drawn by two horses, they rattled
along as Nick Barba drove the Kowalchuk
family through Main Street of Bonnyville and
then southward on a dusty, narrow gravel road
until it stopped at the residence where the
Barba homestead was situated.

The Kowalchuk's definitely needed what
Canada and Bonnyville had to offer – land
and opportunity. As they drove along the
bumpy gravel road the two families discussed
why Roman had to spend time in a lockup,
along with their past and future. Nick Barba
was an interpreter to new Ukrainians and

Poles, and as the driver, looked over his shoulder and casually said to Roman, "Someday I would like to be a politician. Tell me, what is your goal in life now that you are in Canada?"

"Being a farmer, not oppressed by the landlords, giving our children a better life that Evdokia and I had in Ukraine. Even starting from scratch is better than living under Stalin's Communist rule."

Turning towards Pawel, Barba, a revered person, continued, "And you son, what would you like to do when you become an adult?"

Pawel responded with, "Being a politician may be all right but when I grow up I must be what I want to be."

"And what is that?"

"I want to own an inn on the shore of a beautiful lake."

To become an innkeeper in the minds of many Ukrainians meant the acquisition of an honorable place in the community. Inn keeping was an occupation Ukrainians had been virtually excluded from Ukraine now that the country was part of the Communist Soviet Union ruled by Dictator Josef Stalin.

To be able to say, "My son the inn-keeper," gave as much or even more satisfaction as being able to say, "My son the teacher," or "My son the professor."

At any rate Evdokia snapped, "Don't speculate but educate yourself. Study, study my child and then maybe you may reach your goal in life."

Mr. Barba next turned to Kwitka and asked the same question.

"I don't want to live on a farm. I want to be an entertainer," she happily replied.

"Well, I suppose every young girls dream is to be a starlet in Hollywood," Nick Barba said.

As Nick shifted positions and then changed the subject by saying, "And now that the Canadian National Railway is completed from Edmonton to Bonnyville, more Ukrainians are expected in the area. Mark my word, with time, there will be more Slav Europeans around Bonnyville than either than English or French-speaking."

As tough and skilled farmers who knew from experience how to survive on very little, immigrants, like the Kowalchuk's were ideal homesteaders, when they were allowed to be. But most of the time weren't given the chance because most Ukrainians immigrating to Canada were illiterate and disliked by both, Anglos and Francophones.

As a result Ukrainian immigrants were ready for the plucking in their adopted land attracting professional exploiters and confidence men. In Bonnyville it seemed everyone but especially the majority French-speaking, had bargains for them.

"Put your money down," was a common saying by government agents, bank managers, storeowners and agricultural machine companies. And when one day Roman put some down for a lantern, a French-speaking clerk didn't return the proper change and an argument erupted.

In the middle of a heated exchange the clerk said, "Roman Kowalchuk! You are lower in human civilization than an Indian."

Roman, consumed by desire, fought the fire. He wasn't certain if it was the proper thing to do but he was angry, took the chance, and with all the strength, retaliated that day by punching the clerk with a vicious right to the head. That was the reason Roman was serving a three-day jail sentence when Pastor William Aberhart rescued him.

As soon as the Kowalchuk's arrived at the Barba residence, the two families enjoyed a meal of pyrohy, holubtsi and borscht and then stayed up most of the night discussing friends they left behind in the Old Country and how lonely the Barba's were until a new wave of Ukrainian immigrants began to arrive.
The Barba's also talked about their twelve-year-old son, Walter, a tall lanky boy, who enjoyed teasing girls his own age. After having a close look at Kwitka, Olga said, "Walter will make Kwitka an ideal mate once they graduate from high school."
Kwitka upon hearing the remark and not believing in pre-arranged marriages, assured Olga not to make such plans. "No," she reluctantly said, "I'm going to stay single all my life."
Most of the Kowalchuk and Barba relatives and friends lived in villages near Lvov or Kiev in Galicia.

This included Evdokia's sister, Filipa, who married into a middle class family and was a freelance journalist.

Ukrainians were leaving their homeland because of extreme poverty, scarcity of land, and suffering and oppression and discrimination since the rise of totalitarianism in Europe and that part of the turbulent world was sorting itself out after the First World War and the demise of the Austria-Hungarian Empire.

"An economic collapse and famine in Ukraine, part of the Soviet Union, has already claimed millions of lives. Stalin is an absolute Communist dictator four years after Lenin's death," Evdokia said to Olga.

Roman took over, "And Stalin is inaugurating a brutal collectivization program to the Communist Party's advantage. What Stalin is doing to the Ukrainian peasant farmers worries me. I believe there will be millions dead and many more exiled to die in Siberia before the purge is over."

In the morning, it wasn't nine o'clock yet when the Kowalchuk's shed their peasant garb for more practical work clothes and

walked towards their homestead that was
unquestionably flat and where Roman was
building a one-room house with an attached
porch. It was a pleasant dry summer with
raspberries ripening at the edge of the bush,
cranberries turning red, blueberries blue and
saskatoons, pin-cherries and chokecherries
hung in handfuls. As the Kowalchuk's kept
walking partridges and prairie chickens were
near the road, rabbits, gophers and deer
crossed their path and ducks and muskrats,
covered the slough that had a meadow
surrounding it.

There was little time to study wildlife
however, because lot of work had to be done
before the house was completed and winter
set in.

Finally when they reached the house being
built, Evdokia said, "You have been in
Canada one year.  I thought the house would
be completed by now."

"So did I, but there were problems." Roman
said.

Curious, Evdokia asked, "What kind of
problems?"

"I sweated under the sun and fought
mosquitoes as I cleared the trees, dug up roots

and then had the trees delivered to a sawmill to be made into lumber.

For cutting the trees into lumber the sawmill operator as a toll, agreed to keep one- half and I would have the remainder. But do you want to know something?"

"What?" Evdokia said.

"The sawmill operator and I each received a letter from the Director of the Interior, Dominion Lands that our homestead was subject to cancellation proceedings because of my failure to apply for a tree cutting license. I argued that there should be no penalty because I dug the trees, roots and all, out of the ground and furthermore, I had no money at the time."

"And then what happened?"

"I had sixty days to pay the two-dollar fine and when I eventually did, the lumber was recovered and I began building the house."

Evdokia suddenly burst into tears and expressed her first major disappointment since arriving in Canada. She thought the house under construction was okay but the land it stood on was rocky and unproductive.

"Good heavens!" she exclaimed as she bit her lip to stop from shivering. "The land may be

160 acres and costs only $10, but take a look at the landscape.

It's full of rocks and sloughs.

What were you using for eyes when you made claim to this quarter of land?   I'm so disappointed that I feel like returning to Ukraine."

Evdokia was so frustrated that she couldn't speak. Roman did, and what he said was that the fertile homesteads had already been taken by the French-speaking who like Ukrainians, wanted to improve their standard of living.

One of the first problems faced by the Kowalchuk's was educating their children. After centuries of fighting to retain their national identity and having come to Canada under the belief that they could freely do so, the Kowalchuk's also wanted to safeguard their culture and language.

Pawel and Kwitka were enrolled in the one-room Palm Elementary School that was three and one-half miles distant. They often walked with a stick in hand and a lunch pack on their shoulder, cross-country through bushes and fields during summer and snowdrifts three feet deep, even in subzero weather, during winter.

During summer they walked barefoot and were often followed by a pack of coyotes but never did the wild and hungry animals harm them.

The lard or egg sandwiches were packed into a *Gainer or Swift's* lard pail or a ten pound *Roger's* sugar bag. At school the children were always served cocoa.

The children got up early in the morning, have a hardy breakfast of porridge and when they came home in the afternoon the rolled oats was fried and eaten another time until supper was served.

Palm School, like most rural schools at the time, was a one-room wood frame building with plenty of windows on each side. The basic elements of the schoolroom were a table and a chair for the teacher, Miss Cameron, rows of double desks for the students, a blackboard on the front wall, a picture of the King or Queen of England, as applicable, above it, and a Union Jack flag in a front corner. A cast iron wood stove supplied the winter heating.

The teacher arrived early to start a fire in the stove so that the room would be warm and the ink in the inkbottles has melted by the time the students arrived. After grade eight, the students would have to attend Bonnyville High School or drop out of further education. Used to speak Ukrainian at home Pawel and Kwitka at first struggled with the English language and were often teased by older students for being different.

Outside the children played softball, soccer, pump-pump pull -away, anti-eye-over ball and kick-the- can.

Palm School often served as a community Centre. The local families would have dances and social gatherings especially on Friday nights where on many occasions' bootleggers peddled their moonshine.

As the winds of late September began to get colder, Roman took time off from building the house that had no electricity or plumbing, and had Evdokia help him dig a well, which would supply the Kowalchuk's fresh water to drink and used as a refrigerator during the summer.

It was a cool gray day in Bonnyville at the time as Roman had dug all day and about to abandon the project.

"Let's try digging at another location, perhaps, on the other side of the house," Roman suggested.

"No, we aren't finished, dig a bit more," Evdokia urged her husband while looking down a deep hole. "I witched the site with a willow branch like I used to do in the Old Country. There has to be water vein at the bottom."

Evdokia said that ever since she was a child she had a strange sixth sense and a special connection with the earth and its elements. Evdokia was a dowser known also as water diviner or as a water finder.

When Roman doubted the rational he said that Evdokia's gift had not been accepted as scientific evidence that it is effective, she continued, "As a youngster I was able to tell what people were thinking. One day before we were married, I told this to my parish priest Father Shemko."

"And what did the priest say?"

"He told me to focus on the good gift from God, this ability to find water under the parched earth. That is why I'm good at it." What Evdokia had done was to take a cut willow branch that was Y shaped and walk with it back and forth across a clearing.

After walking back and forth for an hour Evdokia's face began turning red and her knuckles turned white, as there was a sudden pull on her hands and into the arms and shoulder. The end of the willow then suddenly plummeted towards the ground, apparently above the water source. That's when Evdokia said, "Roman, this is the spot where we shall continue digging our well."

For another half-day, Roman again swished and swooshed with his spade while Evdokia pulled the dirt in a bucket to the top, but there still was no water. When Roman was about to surrender again, water suddenly began squirting all over. Roman had struck a water vein.

With water up to his knees and rising fast, Evdokia pulled Ed out to safety and then said, "Aha, I told you there was water here."

After Roman had cribbed the well with wood making fresh water available he said to Evdokia, "It's important to help one's neighbor. Why don't you witch a well for Jacques and Yvette Gateau across the road?" "An excellent idea," Evdokia said and away they went to the Gateau residence where they met Jacques Gateau strutting in front of his home like a bantam rooster. And when Evdokia offered Jacques that she could witch a well for him for free, he, without blinking an eyelash, belittled Evdokia's speech, mannerism and dress, and then had the gumption to call Ukrainian immigrants "Scums of Europe."

Several expletive words were exchanged between Roman and the unfriendly neighbor and then, asserting respect, Roman who thought Jacques was acting crazy, rolled up his shirtsleeve and was about to pop Jacques on the nose. Fortunately Evdokia restrained her husband and said, "Roman, please keep your distance and let's go home. We have heard the derogatory phrase before and I'm certain we will hear it many times more."

With that assessment Evdokia was right because the phrase was commonly used by

French and English speaking to describe immigrants from Central and Eastern Europe. As neighbors, the Gateau's and the Kowalchuk's were living opposite each other, actually as well as figuratively.

That night, Roman and Evdokia were filled with guilt that Jacques Gateau did not want to be a friend thus causing discomfort to their neighbor and unhappiness to themselves. Concerned with what had happened, the Kowalchuk's reenacted the incident to the Barba's the same evening.

So Nick Barba  said, to the two immigrants, "Well, one should love his neighbor but in your case maybe by Evdokia offering Jacques to  witch a well for him, was a kind gesture, but on the other hand it could have been a flat-out refusal, and in all likelihood, he probably didn't' set out to be a good neighbor. Maybe he didn't know any better or maybe Jacques was depressed. On the other hand, maybe love is not your thing. Try another direction. Don't say hello to him and if he does say hello to you, pretend you can't hear him.

"At any rate I wouldn't lose any sleep over the incident. Frenchmen like Ukrainians, want to be left alone, preserve their culture, stick to their circle of friends, and if I may say so, some have a tendency to be rude."

"How did you reach that conclusion?" Evdokia asked.

"Well, even in the St. Louis Catholic church, when we attend mass and sit in a pew, invariably a French speaking parishioner comes along minutes later and says, 'Look Hunky, our family has sat in this pew ever since the church was built in 1910 and Father Bonny was the pastor. It best you move over,' and do you want to know something else?"

Curious, Roman said, "What?"

"Sometimes I even wonder if Father Lapointe gives us proper absolution when we go to confession.  It's always the same, five Our Fathers, Five Hail Mary's and one Gloria Be."

The Kowalchuk's were Greek Catholics that used the Byzantine Rite, which was used in Galicia, and also used by Eastern Orthodox churches not in full communion with Rome. These Ukrainians were not Greeks: their religious tradition originated from the Greek

Church in Constantinople, the Capital City of the Eastern Roman Empire and the union between the Bishops of the Metropolia of Kievan Rus' and the Apostolic See. The merger was approved by Pope Clement V111 in 1595 and proclaimed in Brest-Litovsk in 1596. The married priests are permitted to celebrate the Divine Liturgy in Ukrainian and also to baptize, marry and bury. Since the nearest Greek Catholic church was one- hundred miles distance from Bonnyville, in Vegreville, the Kowalchuk's adhered to the Latin Rite.

After discussing Jacques Gateau's rejection and perhaps Father Lapointe's inability to give the correct penance, the two couples played a popular card game in Ukraine called *Holly* and one subject led to another when they discussed the house Roman was building.

"And above all don't forget to build a fire-guard as soon as you can. East central Alberta is ripe for a rip-roaring fire and unless you have a guard, you may be burned out," Nick advised Roman and Evdokia."

By now it was three in the morning and as they continued talking, the northern lights were crisscrossing the sky and coyotes with their haunting sound, howl in the distance.

For the Kowalchuk's their next hurdle was to get the one-room house ready for occupancy. While Roman plastered the building outside with mud and grass, Evdokia did the same inside and then painted the interior with calcimine.

The 18 X 26 foot wood house had a cellar and an attic. The roof was covered with cedar shingles. There was a window in each wall and the front door had a porch over it.

On the feature wall the Kowalchuk's took comfort in the *Last Supper* painting that Evdokia brought from Ukraine.

Calendars from Goldman's General Store and Lee Wong's Royal Chinese Restaurant helped to decorate the interior.

With the decorating done, Roman purchased a wood-burning cooking stove that was placed at one end of the house and a space heater in the centre.

A small door led to the cellar while a ladder leaned against the wall that was used to get inside the attic.

Later, Roman, who was a handyman, built rudimentary cupboards and beds. Pawel and Kwitka slept in the same bed. Roman also made several benches and chairs.

There was no kitchen sink but nearby a pail of water stood on a table, which was covered with a blue-colored oilcloth. Overall the house Roman built wasn't much to endure a harsh winter but still, it was considerably better compared to Barba's first home which was a dugout that provided shelter for their family.

As soon as the house was completed and occupied, Roman built a barn out of logs. It was easier to build than the house had been. The logs were thinner and the barn had a loft where hay could be stored. To have a barn was one of the improvements required before a homesteader received clear title to his property.

Next, Roman built a pigpen followed by a chicken coop and a smoke house where he could cure meat in and since the house had no indoor plumbing, he dug a six-foot deep hole near the barn. Over the hole he built an outhouse, which would serve as a privy.

With most improvements done and winter about to begin, Roman gained employment at a distant sawmill again and would not return home until spring.

It was at the sawmill camp that co-workers were surprised how Roman, who held up his pants with binder twine, could heave and skid logs, pile lumber and sneak up on hibernating bears. On a day when the camp was running short of meat, Roman and a co-worker set out to catch one.

Roman climbed into a bear winter den carrying a flashlight and a snare. The co-worker waited outside with a rope hitched to a team of horses to haul out the animal.

The following day the sawmill employees enjoyed bear meat which some had said tasted better than that of deer or moose.

# CHAPTER 2

By January 1929 it was bitterly cold in
Bonnyville with the temperature plunging to –
40 Fahrenheit, the wind incessantly blowing
and snow drifts up to three feet a common
sight. In the snow, Pawel and Kwitka built
castles and a tunnel that stretched from the
house to the barn. Inside the tunnel they hung
a kerosene lamp, which on one pitch-dark
night led Kwitka to say, "Pawel and I have
created a fantasyland."
It was a time when under-clothing was made
out of flour sacks and the space heater was
filled with wood day and night and the
kerosene lantern turned on as soon as it got
dark. Darkness during the winter came
quickly so the chores had to be done by
approximately 4:00 p. m.

During Roman's absence Kwitka and Pawel
constantly asked, "When is daddy coming
home?"

Each time Evdokia replied, "He'll be coming soon," and complained that she missed Ukraine, was lonely and that the temperature in Bonnyville was more severe than in Siberia.

Evdokia may have been right with that assessment because there were many occasions when Pawel and Kwitka experienced frozen cheeks, nose and toes while walking to and from school.

On extremely cold days, however, the children stayed home and read books. Did arithmetic, English and citizenship lessons.

On one such cold winter day Evdokia asked Pawel, "What grade are you in school?" to which he replied, "Miss Cameron says I'll be in grade three and skip grades as soon as I improve my English and spelling."

Pawel went on to say that each Friday afternoon there was a spelling bee at the school where the girls were on one side and boys on the other. A student sat down as soon as he/she made a spelling mistake. Pawel and Kwitka enjoyed spelling bees and with time, were the last to sit down.

Turning to Kwitka, Evdokia asked the same question

"I'm in grade one and doing fine but I have a problem.

"What is it?"

"Walter Barba, who sits behind me keeps pulling my hair and says I remind him of actress Janet Gaynor in the movie *Street Angel.*"

"I will speak to Walter's mother," Evdokia assured her daughter. "Personally I think Walter is a nice Ukrainian boy."

"Who wears glasses, and has a weird haircut," Kwitka said.


Turning to Pawel Evdokia asked another question which was, "In history what are you studying?"

"We are studying about the Indians, Metis and the Louis Riel Rebellion."

Pawel and Kwitka also discussed with their mother a note from their teacher wondering why Pawel seemed tired while at school.

"Why I'm tired is because I keep thinking about the inn I eventually will build and Miss Cameron has a book reading contest at school.

The student who reads the most books in their grade by the end of the year will win a Kodak Brownie camera," Pawel replied.

In the same note Miss Cameron implied in a subtle way that the Kowalchuk children bathe more often and eat less garlic. "Some children object to that," she wrote.

Miss Cameron's note also suggested that Kwitka might have lice as she had complained about an itchy scalp.

Miss Cameron was correct with that appraisal because lice were a constant problem in school at the time and Kwitka kept scratching her head.

It was while the Kowalchuk family was having supper that one of the lice jumped onto the table. This prompted a family discussion about head lice and for Evdokia to do an inspection of Kwitka's hair where she found little white pearls stuck to the base.

To get rid of the lice, generally associated with dirt, Evdokia had Kwitka soak her hair in vinegar to soften the lice egg and then cover the hair with lard. This done, Kwitka wore a cap overnight and eventually suffocating the ugly bugs.

During the 1929 spring breakup Roman returned home and with the wages earned at the sawmill, purchased a team of horses named *Jenny* and *Prince* and the harness that went with them, a breaking plow to turn over the land and other agricultural equipment that included a sleigh with a box on it.
The horses were the sole means of transportation that the Kowalchuk's had. The following weekend, Roman went to an auction sale in Bonnyville and came back with an assortment of possessions that included a big cross-cut saw for felling trees, an axe for splitting wood, a logging chain that could be used for pulling one out of the mud if one got stuck and for dragging trees out of the bush to be cut into firewood. He also purchased a .22 caliber rifle that could be used to shoot wild animals and birds for food and a dozen traps to catch muskrats.

After cultivating a patch of land near the house, the Kowalchuk's planted potatoes and a vegetable garden that included: lettuce, cucumbers, carrots, turnips, peas and a variety of beans.

There was also dill, which was used in recipes summer and winter along with thyme, mint, sunflower and garlic.

The garden wasn't complete without tomato and cabbage plants that Evdokia seeded in lard and tobacco cans in December making certain the cans were near a window with plenty of light and sunshine. As soon as the plants were three inches tall, Evdokia transplanted them into the garden in a mixture of soil, manure and ashes. She set a tin can around each plant to keep the moisture in and cutworms out.

As soon as the cabbages and tomatoes were planted, Evdokia said to Roman, "When fully grown we'll take the tomatoes to sell at a Farmer's Market in Bonnyville and as for the cabbages, I'll make sauerkraut and cabbage rolls."

Next, Evdokia planted a flower garden on both sides of the 100 foot gravel driveway which when the land was in bloom there would be a myriad of colors: red, pink yellow, white and blue.

Even during winter Evdokia studied a bulb and seed catalogue that Olga had given her, the pages a blur of colors and shapes with tantalizing names like *Purple Pirouette* and *Persian Carpet.*

Evdokia paid attention to the flowering times so that when one color faded another would burst out

As soon as the vegetable and flower gardens were planted, work began clearing a larger parcel of land where first brush had to be cleared and trees pulled and together placed into piles and burned. There were stumps to deal with. Evdokia grubbed the roots and Roman cut them with an axe. After this Jenny and Prince were used to pull out the stumps from the ground one after another.

This done, Roman hitched his team of horses to a walking plow and as he walked behind, furrows unfurled. If the plow suddenly struck a root or a rock Roman would take a tumble but seldom did he get hurt. Roman plowed the earth like there was no tomorrow.

After the parcel of land was broken, roots and rocks had to be picked. Roots were placed into piles and burned while the stones were picked and placed along a boundary fence or where the soil was unfit for cultivation

A stone-boat pulled by the horses was used to get rid of the stones, which each spring seemed to get larger and more plentiful. Disking and harrowing followed until the lumps in the soil were eliminated.
Finally in mid-May Roman planted wheat spreading the kernels by hand because he had not purchased a seed drill as yet. One would follow after more land was cleared and cultivated.
The wheat seeds were purchased from an elevator agent. There were two elevator agents in Bonnyville at the time, one operated by the Searle family from Winnipeg and the other by the Alberta Wheat Pool.
At last, the Kowalchuk's made a proud beginning into the Canadian way of farming and would wait until September to enjoy the fruits of his labor.

In the meantime, Evdokia spent more time on her knees during June and July than rest of the liturgical year. There was good reason to pray: a blight of cabbage butterflies and cut worms.  But when Evdokia was in that bowed-down position she was not always praying but weeding the garden.

If there were a patron saint for weeds she would pray to him/her too as Evdokia tried everything else. She hoed, raked, clipped and burned

Nothing worked, especially on the quack grass and dandelions that grew rampantly and each subsequent crop was more varied and luxuriant than the first.

On the plus side, however, Evdokia made crowns and wreaths and chains out of the yellow-colored blossoms. Another use for dandelion leaves was in salads, Roman making wine and Evdokia an instant devotee when the weather was favorable. When it came to weather forecasting farmers in those days did not have satellites or weather forecasters. They relied on the sky, winds and clouds.

Eventually patterns emerged and the homesteaders made up sayings to remember them.  Here are several time-tested sayings with the meteorological reasoning to back them up.

1. Red sky in the morning, take warning. Red sky at night, farmer's delight
2. Hens scratching dirt, with rain a farmer will flirt
3. Summer fog will scorch a hog
4. When the dew is on the grass, rain will never come to pass
5. A strong north wind says a storm is nigh. A strong west wind will clear the sky
6. A drop in the barometer pressure, lousy weather. Headaches and a circle around the sun, cold weather will come
7. A bright full moon, favorable weather will come
8. Seagulls flying in a flock, bad weather for the stock
9. A cat or dog eating grass, a storm will pass.

# CHAPTER 3

Aside from improving the property, Roman had ordered a bundle, which was advertised in the *Western Producer* newspaper. The Kowalchuk's were in their glory when the bundle arrived and found clothing inside to fit most members of the family.

They were disappointed, however, that there were no shoes and Pawel and Kwitka had to walk barefoot to school. It was during the school's annual picnic that Kwitka, because lack of footwear, stepped on an anthill and her feet became swollen and red in color.

The ant bites did not bother Kwitka however, as she won first prize ribbons in the broad and high jumps. Kwitka was proud of her accomplishments and so were her parents. With warmer weather Roman continued making improvements to the homestead by building a barbed wire fence around the homestead while Evdokia and the children picked wild berries and mushrooms, when they could.

As for the wild berries, first there were wild strawberries in July followed by raspberries, saskatoons, cranberries, pin- cherries, gooseberries and chokecherries
Out of the berries, Evdokia made preserves and pies, out of the rose whips, marmalade and sauce, out of the pin-cherries and chokecherries Roman made wine.

Growing up on a homestead when hunger often stared the immigrant in the face, the Kowalchuk's soon learned to depend on the bounties of the woods and meadows. As for mushrooms, from May until fall, after every rain, the delicacies seemed to spring out from the ground within hours. The rule in picking the right mushroom was, if in doubt, leave them alone. At any rate mushrooms were good to eat. Served with gravy they were delicious and helped round out a meal. Those that weren't eaten were dried and eaten later or else, like the wild berries, sold in bucketful's to the Goldman General Store that was situated on Main Street in Bonnyville.

The store was a white colored wood-frame
building with a red-shingled roof and the
paint peeling. A *Coca Cola* sign on the
exterior was the real thing. Inside oiled
floorboards smelled of linseed oil.

Goldman's General Store did not sell slurpes,
submarine sandwiches or soft ice cream
because they were unknown at the time. Back
then the store sold animal feed, fuel, clothing
and groceries. The interior featured hand-
written signs advertising goods found on
wooden shelves.
There was no surveillance system because
Abraham Goldman lived upstairs and
shoplifting was rare. There were no air miles
or discount coupons. The store was unique
and had an atmosphere where customers
would meet and also socialize. Most of the
homesteaders did their shopping on a
Monday. The teams of horses were either tied
to a wooden fence or fed at a private livery
barn where in the middle stood a large wheel
and a dog inside that was used to pump water
into a trough. The dog always seemed to
enjoy its work.

Jewish merchants like Goldman's, were principally immigrants from Eastern Europe and by now there seemed to be a *Jew Store* in nearly every Canadian town.

The Jewish immigrant was no different from peasants he used to trade with in Poland, Russia and Ukraine.

What the Jewish merchant like Goldman did was completely devoid of politics, idealism, paternalism and charity.

He was interested only in making a profit and expanding his business. Among the unusual problems of being Jewish in a community like Bonnyville however, was to maintain his dietary rules under frontier conditions.

It was a time in Canadian history where the Anglo Saxon population referred to Slavs as *Bohunks* who were dumb and lousy, the Chinese were referred as Chinks that smoked opium and robbed graves, Italians were Dagos who carried knifes, Jews as Hebes and Black people as Niggers and the French-speaking as "Frogs" and "Peasoupers."

That summer Evdokia and the children picked and sold enough wild berries enabling them to order clothing and footwear for winter through Eaton's and Simpson's catalogues, which in a farmer's home, seemed to be almost as important as the *Bible*. When the catalogues expired their pages were used as toilet paper in the outhouse.

Improvements to the farm were done despite an abundance of mosquitoes and black flies. Since the Kowalchuk's lived near a slough and a creek July rain and wind storms drove up mosquito numbers.

The Kowalchuk's were told that mosquitoes were attracted more to Ukrainians than to those who spoke English of French was because of the bright colored clothing they wore. In order to get rid of the sting due to mosquito bites the Kowalchuk's rubbed their face and arms with cloves of garlic. Everyone had his or her favorite repellent. Some swore by it and others swore at it. Even burning smudges seemed to increase the mosquito attacks that at one point, while Evdokia was weeding the garden and had a smudge going, led her to say, "I wish the wind would blow the blood suckers in the direction of the Jacques Gateau residence."

Somehow Evdokia's wish was granted because on a quiet evening, while Roman was absent, the wind suddenly changed direction and drove the smoke towards the Gateau property.

Seeing and smelling the smoke, Jacques rushed to its source and after ranting and raving vehemently called Evdokia a, "Russian Bohunk."
"Stop croaking, like a frog!" Evdokia retorted and slammed the door in Jacque's face.
Since that time Jacques came to despise the senior Kowalchuk's and embarked on a lifetime of secretly scheming against them.

Evdokia lost her temper another time too when a deer came and while in the garden began munching the cabbage plants.
"Oh, my God! What will I use for my cabbage rolls?" Evdokia said to Pawel, grabbed the rifle her husband had bought, aimed, and seemingly shot the deer.
While bent over the animal to see if there was a prospect of venison, the deer suddenly sprang to its feet and began running with Evdokia on its back.

This was one ride Evdokia wished she never had because the deer bucked and Evdokia fell to the ground. Mind you being bucked off a deer was no big deal but unfortunately Evdokia was pregnant at the time with her third child.

The following week, Evdokia had another terrifying experience when the Barba's arrived unexpectedly and she attempted to behead a hen for supper. Halfway through the process of wringing her neck the hen fought its way loose and fled running around in circles.
Pawel had to catch her and use an axe to chop off the head on a block of wood.

Once the hen was stripped of its feathers that were used in making quilts and pillows, the chicken was cut into pieces that were rolled in flour and placed into a frying pan. The dinner was delicious but something must be said about the hen that was eaten. Whenever company dropped by she had the habit of popping inside the house every time Evdokia opened the door.

Evdokia had to shoo her out constantly, and at mealtime the hen was a hazard. Grasshoppers, which she had to catch herself, were her only source food and thus she was constantly hungry. Often the hen flew onto the kitchen table and snatched pieces of pyrohy or holubtsi out of Evdokia's hand.

One day the hen was nearly roasted however. At that time Evdokia had gone to weed the garden. When she came back the wind had blown the door wide open and there was the hen stuck deep in a batch of fresh bread dough cackling for help.

With the agricultural process beginning in earnest and still having some cash on hand Roman purchased a red cow that would provide milk, cream, cheese and butter for the family. Roman said the cow was sort of wild but would soon get over her wildness and be gentle as a kitten.
Evdokia was pleased with the cow but her pleasure was short lived, because after the pretty beast was lead to the barn and Evdokia affronted her to milk, she unexpectedly lifted her tail and galloped throughout the barn

upsetting the milk pail, the chickens got frightened and Pushka, the dog, began barking.

"Oh, what a day this has been," Evdokia said. As soon as Roman corralled the cow and placed her into a stall, she refused to eat hay and chew the cud, she even stopped giving milk. Instead of straightening out the poor creature, Roman slaughtered her for meat to eat and purchased another cow to supply the Kowalchuk family with milk.

During the 1929 winter, Roman spent more time at the lumber camp and when he returned in the spring with cash on hand, he drove to town alone, and at an auction sale where for a bargain price successfully bid on a radio and a gramophone with 100 cylinder-shaped records. As soon as he returned home Evdokia questioned his purchase.

"Why did you buy a radio and a gramophone at a time when there are more important things the family needs?" she said, her voice trembling.

"Oh," Roman said nonchalantly, "I bought both because it was a great deal and number one, I want to listen to Bible Bill Aberhart on the *Back To The Bible* program from Calgary and two, the radio will help us to keep abreast of news from throughout the world. The radio will also help us to improve our English when we apply to become British subjects."

"And the Edison gramophone?" Evdokia then asked.

"I'll answer that," Kwitka cut in. "I can sing along with some of the records and perhaps eventually become a celebrity."

Pawel said he would enjoy both, the radio and the gramophone, because he enjoyed listening to news bulletins and popular music.

Pawel already had memorized names of every Canadian prime minister, provincial capitals and important historical dates since Confederation. He also said that he would enjoy the *Amos n Andy* program that hit the airwaves recently.

By now Kwitka had one of the cylinders on the gramophone. She checked the diamond needle and wound up the machine. The tune was *Spring Time in the Rockies* by Wilf Carter.

As soon the record finished playing she slapped on another and as the gramophone played *Marian Anderson*, Kwitka sang with her*, Ave Maria.*

"And do you want to know something else? Roman said.

Evdokia smiled, "That someday you'll buy me a piano."

"You can count on that. Someday soon, I hope." Roman said.

During the summer of 1929 Roman and Jacques vowed not to say kind words about each other. They avoided each even when crossing paths in downtown Bonnyville or while shopping at Goldman's General Store or at Brousseau's, Valleee's or Kowalski's. Although the parents avoided each other, their children didn't. One evening while having pyrohy for supper Pawel said that he and Gloria Gateau spent some time playing in the hayloft and that Gloria's parents, like his, are devout Catholics.

"If I ever catch you and Gloria in the hayloft again, you'll get a whipping like you never had," Evdokia warned her son.

"I know that while in the hayloft you and Gloria weren't reciting the rosary."

"But Mom," Pawel protested, "Just because the parents do not speak to each other, doesn't mean their children can't be friends."

During September the Kowalchuk's were huddled around the radio listening to Reverend Aberhart who was compared to Father James Coughlin and his sermons on national justice originating from Detroit.

After the Kowalchuk's had listened to the Aberhart sermon and then gone to bed, an unusual thing for east central Alberta happened overnight.

Frost destroyed their crop although the ground vegetables and potatoes were salvaged. Like many families, the Kowalchuk's' grew a large potato and cabbage patch.

It was a time when Roman was now short of money and since bank credit cards weren't yet available, there was no one he could turn to as most of the other homesteaders were in the same predicament.

It was a matter of fighting for survival and the only consolation the Kowalchuk's had was faith, that they had picked enough wild berries during summer to be preserved in glass jars and stored in the cellar, and that the potatoes could be used as a sort of currency, bartering for services when cash wasn't available. As an example when a bill arrived from the St. Louis Hospital in the amount of $15 Roman paid $5.00 in cash and the balance in potatoes which were dug with a hoe, picked off the ground, placed into gunny sacks and taken to the hospital in a wagon or sleigh drawn by a team of horses.

On October 28th Roman and Evdokia had their first Canadian born child but the birth process was a difficult one. Can one imagine giving birth in a brand new country while one was dealing with culture shock, language barriers, resentment and loneliness?
There were no pre-natal classes; money was in short supply and childbirth customs exotic and bizarre to Canadian doctors and nurses. The more an immigrant woman asked questions, the more stupid the doctors and nurses would think she was.

The hospital in Bonnyville was new and run by the Grey order of nuns and Dr, Severyn Sabourin who was anxious to show it off to the public - shiny walls, the white iron cots and the deadly aroma of ether and *Lysol*. But even during early stages of her pregnancy Evdokia let it be known that, "I would rather have my child born at home than at the hospital."

The baby was two weeks premature and Evdokia said to Roman while in pain, "I don't know if being a victim of a deer bucking me off has anything to with the trouble or not but the baby has difficulty in coming out. Please ask Olga Barba to come and help."
Evdokia took Roman by the hand as she lay on the bed.
"Never, I will deliver the child myself," Roman replied as he gave his wife's hand a squeeze and then picked up a clean towel and placed a kettle full of water on the kitchen stove to boil. When Evdokia's pain got stronger and contraction periods shorter, Evdokia insisted that Roman call Olga and have her come over.

The bed was already bloodstained and Evdokia's long black hair fell over her face as she crouched again, to no avail. Seeing Evdokia was pale and in excruciating pain Roman finally relented and said, "Okay I'll go and bring Olga so she can help you."

Roman ran as fast as his legs could carry him to the Barba residence to impart the news that Evdokia was having a premature baby. Olga loved going over to the Kowalchuk's because Evdokia was her best friend. And when she did arrive, the baby's head emerged. It had dark hair, the same as Evdokia's and Roman's.
Then Evdokia said, "The baby won't come further."

Olga sobbed in anguish and said, "Come on Evdokia!  It's coming, push again!" But Evdokia was too weak to try and as the pain subsided. Olga realized what was wrong. The baby was facing up instead of down and they would have to turn it. Olga had done it with calves during calving season in the spring and she had assisted her husband.

Olga quickly turned to Roman and explained the problem. She knew that if the baby wasn't turned it might die or Evdokia would. Another pain ripped through Evdokia and this time Olga didn't tell Evdokia to push instead she gently pressed her own hands into Evdokia and felt the baby in her womb.
Another pain came and Evdokia pushed again to force Olga from her, but Olga withdrew her hands and the head moved further again.
Suddenly Evdokia pushed as though she never could have. The baby began to emerge and Olga gave a shout of victory as the head came out and then rest of the baby.

Tears came down Olga's cheeks as she worked to free Evdokia and her baby and then there was a tense silence in the room as the baby began crying.
It was a baby boy. The placenta came afterward which Roman disposed in a grove of pine trees.
It was washed and buried in a secret shady place. If this ritual wasn't performed correctly Roman believed Evdokia and the baby could become very sick and even die.

"Thank you, thank you," Evdokia said. She was too tired to say much more and closed her eyes as she held baby Nicholas to her breast and Roman and Olga watched as milk, white as snow, gushed forth.

"Olga, I think you saved Evdokia's life. Thank you again," Roman then said.

"You are welcome," Olga replied and as she was making her exit Roman continued, "This is a day I shall never forget."

Next day, October 29, 1929, was a day the entire world would remember too – the New York stock market crashed on a Black Tuesday turning the Roaring Twenties into Hungry Thirties. There were hundreds of suicides. With the collapsing of Wall Street the stock market began the greatest depression in American and Canadian history.

The world was in turmoil and the local price of wheat dropped by more than 50% and lumber and newsprint by forty.

Financial gloom kept spreading and an indication of prevailing economic conditions was the appearance of apple vendors on street corners singing *Hallelujah I'm a Bum* and *Brother Can You Spare a Dime?*

Bootleg prices of liquor were high. Canadian rye sold for $150.00 a case, Scotch $110 and moonshine was prevalent everywhere.
The value of Canada's agricultural exports fell from $783-million to $253-million.
The markets for Canadian goods had dried up. Cattle sold for 3.5 to 4 cents a pound, potatoes 15 cents for a 90-pound bag and in British Columbia 8000 tons of tomatoes and orchard fruit were plowed under.

The *Dirty Thirties Depression* lasted until World War 11 began in 1939 so the Kowalchuk's, like most immigrant families during that period, struggled to survive and prosper.
They battled poverty, storms, crop failures, blizzards, mosquitoes and grasshoppers, the hardship of homesteading, ethnic prejudice and homesickness in the new Promised Land.

It was a time when radio was reaching over oceans, continents and hemispheres. In east central Alberta, at nighttime, one could pick up KGA Spokane, KOA Denver, KSL Salt Lake City, and even XRE Del Rio, Texas that advertised a variety articles including mufflers for cars, remedies for headaches and pictured Bibles for children.

The most listened to stations in Bonnyville however, were CKUA and CFRN in Edmonton and CFCN in Calgary. An estimated 150-million people listened to Britain's Prime, Minister Ramsay MacDonald, say, "Truly we are living in times of great miracles."
"I wish we were," Roman said to Evdokia, Pawel and Kwitka who were also listening to the broadcast at the time.

It was a time when over 20,000 listeners in the Prairie Provinces, the interior of British Columbia and the state of Montana listened regularly to Aberhart's program *Back to the Bible Hour.*
It was a time in history when the Canadian population was ten-million and no work was available and with the Depression catching hold with a tighter grip; Roman decided to stay at home and in November suggested how the family could survive.
Curious, Evdokia said, "How?"

"We have a team of horses and a sleigh and…"

"And what?"

"And sell cords of wood to the residents and merchants of Bonnyville."

Evdokia thought selling wood for furnaces and space heaters was a splendid idea and cheaper than coal. She offered to help when, "Nicholas doesn't need my attention."

During the harsh and cruel winter, where the temperature often fell to F40 below and the wind blew incessantly, Roman and Evdokia cut down dried spruce, poplar and birch trees. They didn't cut tamarack trees because its wood was ideal for making fence posts.

With a team of horses they dragged the trees to a spot near the house where a sawhorse was built. Once the branches were removed the couple sawed and split trees most of the day. When Pawel and Kwitka returned home from school, they too helped and placed each piece of sawed wood into a cord measurement and then into the sleigh box.

The following morning, Roman put on his
sheepskin coat and felt leather boots, hitched
the horses to a sleigh and drove eight miles to
Bonnyville with his first load of wood. As
soon as he reached a particular street or
avenue he hollered, "Firewood for sale! You
can have your pick – spruce, poplar or birch!"
The customers Roman encountered were
mostly French-speaking and when they
ridiculed his Ukrainian accent, Roman had a
standby response that was, "I'm sorry I can't
speak good English but hope you realize the
English speaking mimic your accent too."
In most cases Roman's wood got sold, even
Lee Wong at the Royal Chinese Restaurant
and Abe Goldman's General Store gave him
repeat orders.
With the money earned the Kowalchuk's
bought the necessities to sustain life: flour,
lard, yeast, coal oil, salt and oatmeal.
Closer to Christmas they also purchased a box
of Okanagan apples, Florida oranges, a can of
peanut butter and a small barrel of herring.
There were also treats for Pawel and Kwitka,
candy.

Relationship with the Goldman General Store grew to a point where Goldman offered the Kowalchuk's, a line of credit.

"You are honest and hardworking people," Goldman said after he bought a load of wood. "My parents were poor too when they arrived from Russia, lived in Winnipeg and were smeared with anti-Semitism by Anglo Saxons and the French."

Goldman's General Store was a gathering place for European immigrants and Goldman said that when news reached him that a railway line was about to be completed to Bonnyville and the immigration of Europeans was about to explode to the area, he purchased the store from the previous owner whose specialty was buying animal furs from the Indians.

One day Roman, was sitting near a space heater at the centre of the store while Goldman was straightening and dusting around the only cash register, when Roman casually said," Mr. Goldman, you are still single, how come?"

"I am but at one time I had a fiancé who was a French-speaking Catholic."

"And what happened? She got killed in a car accident?"

"No, I took my parents' advice to discontinue the relationship and when we did, she took vows and became a nun. To tell you the truth her departure from my life is unbearable, I loved her so much."

"That's a pity. I'm sorry."

Just then a Black customer by the name of Josiah Alexander, who worked on the railroad and enjoyed the sport of boxing, entered the store in his working overalls and in a semi-circle sat next to Roman.

Alexander was followed by 41-year-old Chief Joe Dion from the nearby Kehewin Indian Reserve who wore an embroidered buckskin jacket, no feathers sticking out of his hair that was long and braided but wasn't as dangerous as those in Europe were led one to believe. Dion was son of Gustav Dion a Metis, and Marion Dion, a Cree. He married Elizabeth Cunningham of St. Albert in 1912, educated; he was a teacher of note at the reserve a short distance south of Bonnyville. After some front talk Chief Dion asked Roman the inevitable, "Why did you come to Canada?"

The answer was, "For a brighter future for my children and freedom to enjoy."

Turning to Alexander the Chief asked, "And you, Josiah, what made you come to Bonnyville?"

Alexander hesitated for a second, although he was asked the same question many times by his neighbors. His ancestry stemmed from the California Gold Rush where his parents suffered racial discrimination. Negroes couldn't give evidence in a California court against White people nor could they attend a White school.

"Our people were bullied and maltreated in California so my parents moved to Victoria, British Columbia. But even there we were barred from theatres and bars so my family and I moved to Bonnyville where eventually I found employment on the railroad."

When Alexander was asked what he thought of Canada he replied, "Well, it's the best poor man's country that I know."

Both Roman and Alexander were curious about Bonnyville's history. It took courage but Roman turned to Chief Dion and asked, "Who was the first White man in the area?"

Chief Dion did not hesitate, "He was a fur trader by the name of Angus Shaw who came to Moose Lake in 1870. Shaw was probably the first White man the Cree Indians in the area dealt with."

Chief Dion went on to say that it wasn't until 1906 when fur bearing animals became extinct in Eastern Canada that a hunter/trapper by the name of Charles Lirette, arrived from Massachusetts after reading an advertisement over the signatures of two Oblate priests, Father Joseph Therien and J. A. Oullette, urging people in the province of Quebec and Eastern United States to colonize east-central Alberta.

"From time immemorial my people depended on this area for their livelihood," Chief Dion said.

"From time immemorial?" Alexander quipped, "I always thought since Creation, God allowed this part of Canada only to the French."

Roman said he'd like to hear more so the Chief continued, "I have many word accounts of happy days spent after the trappers had brought home successful catches of fox, ermine, mink, muskrats, coyote and of course, beaver."

Halfway through the conversation Goldman asked, "Is it true there were lean periods too?"

"There were lean periods of course but our people never starved."

"I hope we don't have to starve through the economic conditions we are presently in," Goldman broke in and went on, "But tell me Chief, what was the 1870 epidemic like?"

"That's a different story. You may be surprised but thank the Great Spirit my parents survived.

Chief Dion then recalled how on the dark day in Canadian Indian history the epidemic struck fast, wiping out entire families.

Hearing this Goldman shifted slightly and asked another question, "And the Great Famine of 1872, what was it like?"

"The famine wasn't heavily felt because through hunting and fishing Indians were able to find food to eat."

"It wasn't like the forced famine that presently is taking place in Ukraine?" Roman asked.

"I didn't know that there is one."

"I suppose your people participated in the massacre at Frog Lake during the Louis Riel Rebellion in 1885?" Goldman went on but this time Chief Dion shook his head. "They didn't although my people were interested in what Riel was trying to achieve."

Near the end of the chit-chat Alexander was blunt and to the point, "Tell me Chief, as an Indian, what was your people's greatest mistake?"

"In Canada or Bonnyville?"

"Bonnyville."

Chief Dion thought for a moment. Once his thought crystallized, he said, "A regrettable incident from our point of view took place when officials of the Department of Indian Affairs had called a meeting at which they advised Indians to avail themselves to treaty money and a reservation of their own near Moose Lake but it didn't happen."

"Why not?"

"Because Indians scoffed at the idea of being tied down to a parcel of land that originally belonged to them. Indians refused to heed the warning that Bonnyville would soon be filled with White people.

Indians felt there was room for everyone no matter what language one spoke or the color of their skin."

Seconds later, the Chief said that before he became Chief of the Kehewin Reserve a treaty was signed with the Canadian government stipulating that their treaty money was to be paid as long as nearby Muriel Lake assured them a source fish and water. The summer that he became Chief there was a terrible draught however, and the lake became shallow and dwindled to its lowest level ever, and thus Indians could not safely anchor their boats anymore, as the nearest water was five-hundred feet from shore. Alarmed, Indians came from as far as Cold Lake, Saddle Lake and even Hobbema. They gathered at the lakeshore and together with the Chief and his family, prayed to the Great Spirit to send rain. The Great Spirit heard their plea and the following day there was a downpour and the treaty money was saved.

Although the Kowalchuk's practiced the Latin Catholic rite Father Wasyil Bodnar visited his Greek Catholic flock in and near Bonnyville during Easter and Christmas periods to offer blessings and take confessions in their native language.

It was several days before Christmas Eve that the elderly priest arrived in a cutter pulled by horse from Vegreville at the Kowalchuk residence.
One reason for the visit of course, was that Father Lapointe did not understand the Ukrainian language and for absolution always gave his confessors five *Hail Mary's*, five *Our Father's* and a *Gloria Be* as a penance.
"As for eating meat on a Friday, don't worry about that because times are getting tough. Not eating meet on a Friday of course, keeps your grocery bill down," Father Bodnar said.
After socializing for an hour Evdokia took a blanket from a bed and suspended it from the ceiling, after which Father Bodnar sat on a chair and took confessions from each member of the family.
Father Bodnar could not stay for a taste of Roman's chokecherry wine because a weather forecast showed a snowstorm was brewing and he still had three more families to visit before it got dark.

As the Kowalchuk's began to assimilate into society they maintained many Ukrainian traditions practiced in Ukraine but not Canada. One was to throw a spoonful of *kutya* towards the ceiling. The more it stuck to the ceiling, the better the crop would be next year. As soon as Father Bodnar finished taking confessions, he shook hands with members of the family. Even baby Nicholas received attention as Father Bodnar said to him, "Kootchy, kootchy koo. Merry Christmas to you too."

As soon as the handshaking was done, Father Bodnar, whose horse was tied to a fence post and fed with chop, hopped into the cutter and drove away but not before complimenting Evdokia on her baking and said, "Looks like the kutya didn't stick to the ceiling which means a tough winter lies ahead. God bless the Kowalchuk family and Merry Christmas to everyone."

That Christmas Eve the Kowalchuk's did not attend midnight mass because as Father Bodnar had predicted earlier, there was a blizzard brewing. The northeast wind was up to fifty miles an hour and snowdrifts three feet deep. All the roads in and around Bonnyville were blocked. The storm first struck in the late afternoon knocking down trees and closing businesses. At the height of the storm Bonnyville was without electricity and people played cards and monopoly by candlelight or a kerosene lamp. The storm seemed to bring families together but not Roman Kowalchuk and Jacques Gateau.

The Kowalchuk's did find comfort however, because as they were going to bed they listened on the radio to a live broadcast of Pope Pius X1 saying mass from the Vatican.

On Christmas day the Kowalchuk's exchanged gifts they made for each other: scarves, mitts, sweaters and toys cut out of wood. Kwitka's favorite was a doll trunk her father made out of an orange box. It had tiny brass hinges that Kwitka at first thought was made out of pure gold.

The kitchen was still filled with the aroma of Evdokia's freshly baked bread. Baking bread was a two-day project that began several days before Father Bonder's visit. At that time Evdokia crumbled a yeast cake into lukewarm water and let it soak in a warm place that afternoon. That evening, using a wooden box she made a starter batter of flour and water and the fully dissolved yeast mixture. The box was wrapped into a down-filled quilt and set to rise overnight on the kitchen table. In the morning Evdokia added salt and flour to the bubbling batter. Then she kneaded the soft dough until it was smooth. She wrapped the quilt around the box and set the dough to rise in a warm spot near the stove. Two hours later, when the dough doubled in size, she punched it down gently and let it rise again. As soon as the dough had risen, Evdokia shaped it into loaves and let them rise, covered with tea towel, in a warm draft-free place. Before placing the bread pans into the oven, she dipped a feather brush into an egg wash and swished it over each loaf.

During the summer, Evdokia usually baked bread in a pre-heated oven outside. Pawel and Kwitka gathered wood to build a roaring fire inside the oven.
When the fire was reduced to glowing red embers, Evdokia raked them out and tossed in a handful of corn meal.

If the particles jumped when they hit the clay floor, the oven was ready to take the loaves. When the oven was fully loaded, Evdokia closed the wooden door and propped it shut with a short wooden pole.

During the hour-long baking, she checked on how fast the bread was browning. If the clay oven was too hot, she removed the metal can covering the hole at the back of the oven, allowing some heat to escape.

Kwitka always knew when the bread was done. Back and forth Pawel and Kwitka rushed carrying the shiny, golden crusty loaves into the house. Evdokia's reward was watching faces as her children feasted on thick slices of warm bread spread with freshly churned butter and a glass of milk to drink.

# CHAPTER FOUR

As soon as the festive season was over and 1930 arrived, Roman discovered that he had competition in that Jacques Gateau had an abundance of trees on his homestead and with his wife, decided to cut, split and sell firewood to the merchants and residents of Bonnyville, like Roman did. Rivalry between Jacques and Roman became so intense that each rose 5:00 a. m. – 20 below outside to feed and harness their team of horses. Then one morning while Jacques and Roman were racing towards Bonnyville with a load of fire wood, their sleighs fell through the ice of Jessie Lake that was used for a winter short cut.
Even then the two neighbors did not speak to each other, their personalities collided again as they returned home on foot to ask their wives to help.

When Roman wasn't selling fire wood and was idle, Chief Dion showed him how to make pemmican and bannock and hunt animals and birds for food: deer, partridges and prairie chicken which were better tasting than ducks were.

Their flesh was dark and their legs full of tendons but the breasts were thick and juicy, especially when rolled in flour and fried in grease.

"Fit for a king, aren't they?" Roman said. Pointing to Evdokia he continued, "I bet you never had a meal like that in Ukraine."

Chief Dion also showed young Pawel how to trap fur bearing animals during winter: muskrat, weasel, squirrel, and coyote and to snare white rabbits with a piece of copper wire. Pawel checked his mini-trap line each morning before going to school.

As for the rabbits he would skin them and then stretch the pelt on a thin board in the barn to dry. As soon as he had fifty pelts he packed them into a paper box and delivered them to Goldman's General Store where they were sold at five cents each. As for the rabbit carcasses they were tossed into the pigpen for the hogs to enjoy, and if they didn't, crows and magpies did.

But above all the things Chief Dion showed Roman was the clear element, with no cruelty intended, how to properly shoot and clean a deer that were plentiful at the time.

"You may shoot one for food. Nothing else," the Chief said.

After shooting a doe, Roman brought it home, where the animal was cleaned and venison was about to be served for supper. Roman knew that Kwitka and Pawel were fussy eaters and wouldn't eat wild meat if told what it was. Kwitka however, kept bugging him, "What's for supper, Dad?"

"You'll see as soon as it it's done.  It's in the oven at the moment."

When the venison roast was placed on the table and supper began, Kwitka brought a piece to her mouth and after tasting it said, "Dad.  What are we eating?"

"Okay," Roman said.  "Here's a hint. It's what your mother sometimes calls me."

Kwitka screamed, "Hey Mom!  Hey Pawel! Stop eating!" One of the first English words she learned at school was, "It's an asshole!"

During the summer, the Kowalchuk homestead wasn't Capistrano and the birds weren't swallows. What happened was that a huge flock of crows kept returning to the neighborhood. The big, black, noisy birds had been calling the area during the summer leaving their messing calling cards on rooftops, clotheslines, fence posts and machinery.

The crows spread out to the fields during daytime and in the evening returned to roost in yards in a cawing black cloud that darkened the sky. Roman complained not only about the cawing noise and destruction of his crop, but also expressed concern about the state of the family health and environment.

"Why our children should be playing in crow droppings?" he said to Evdokia.

The Kowalchuk's first tried scaring the crows by banging pots and pans, setting up scare crow in fields and even putting artificial owls on trees but nothing worked.

Crows are scavengers eating road kill and garbage but they also hunt for food.

"They'll eat just about anything," Roman protested to Pawel.

That includes insects, frogs, worms, eggs, mice and even smaller birds."

When Pawel saw a crow attack a blue jay, he said to his father, "I know how to get rid of the crows."

Carious to know, Roman asked, "How?"

"Let's shoot them,"

"Go ahead," Roman said and handed his 13-year-old son the 22 gauge rifle.

Within one day Pawel shot fifty crows and twenty magpies, cut off their legs and sold them to the Goldman General Store for a bounty of one-cent a leg.

There was also a gopher-tail bounty that year where one got paid three cents a tail before May 15, two cents after. When it came to the gophers whose population, like the rabbits', ran in cycles of abundance and scarcity, Pawel chased the rodents and poured water down a hole and finally pegging each as it stuck out its head, with a rifle shot.

Shooting gophers was a sort of sport but the rodents weren't as stupid as it seemed. When they were chased they ran but only a short distance. The moment Pawel came a little too close; they popped down a convenient a hole, flicking their tails mockingly.

Pawel decided not to sell their tails after May 15th but become an entrepreneur and operate what he called, "My toy gopher boutique." Pawel continued shooting gophers but since he was unfamiliar with taxidermy he removed the inside and stuffed the rodents with newspapers. With Kwitka's help he dressed the animals to look like Jacques Gateau, Abe Goldman, Father Lapointe and Lee Wong. Once the gophers were attired Pawel brought them to the end of the driveway and placed them in line by the front gate. A hand written sign next to the gophers read: *Pawel Kowalchuk's Gopher Hole Boutique.* Underneath the sign were the words, *50 Cents Each.*

Pawel sat on a chair and waited. After an hour not a single vehicle or a team of horses drove by but Pawel was determined to stay until one did.

Seeing their son sitting alone his parents walked down to the driveway and when they reached Pawel, Evdokia said, "How is it going?"

"Good."

Roman looked at the gophers and then the sign.

"Nobody will buy a gopher for fifty cents,"

"Dad, watch and see, they eventually will."

"But there isn't enough traffic here. Why don't you get rid of the gophers and go and play?"

"But there are. I see cars and teams of horses passing every day."

Having failed to convince Pawel of the futility of his efforts the parents returned to the house and watched through a window. Minutes later a car with a man inside drove by. The driver craned his neck and after reading the sign backed up his vehicle, walked up to Pawel and said, "Please, I'll have two of your stuffed gophers."

After Pawel was given one-dollar he said to the stranger, "Haven't I seen you somewhere before?"

"You may. I'm Andre Nadeau, editor of the Bonnyville *Nouvelle* newspaper. And you are?"

"Pawel Kowalchuk. Glad to meet you, sir"

"And do you want to know something else?" Nadeau continued.

"What, sir?"

"I'm going to write an article that will include photographs about your gophers in next week's edition."

Nadeau, after taking snapshots of the dressed gophers, picked up a pad from his car and then to Pawel said, "Where do I begin?" The newspaperman wrote about the stuffed gophers and how the idea originated. He also wrote about Pawel's marketing plan for the stuffed rodents, which included T-shirts, garden planters and birdhouses, all with a gopher theme.

The following week the *Nouvelle* indeed did carry an article and a photograph about Pawel's Gopher Hole Boutique giving the venture a lot of publicity. Customers drove from Bonnyville to the Kowalchuk homestead and as far away as St. Paul, Grand Centre and Cold Lake. Without exception customers described the stuffed gophers as *cuties*. During the night when the weather was inclement Pawel stored his gophers into an empty granary. But even before the article appeared in the newspaper Gloria became emotional about nature denouncing the stuffed gophers and said to Pawel, "What gives you the right to kill gophers that haven't even begun to live lives yet? Can't you see the cute animals have spirits like we do? Gophers are creatures created by God." Pointing her finger at one of the rodents she continued, "And look at that gopher, you made it like my father."

Pawel told Gloria to go and stuff herself and pointed out that gophers destroy crops, invite predators like the badger who dig huge, dangerous holes, large enough for one to fall in and break a leg. And then he went on to say that farmers kill gophers anyway and that his boutique was similar to a museum that educates people.

At any rate what difference does it make, to use gophers this way or let them rot in the field?" Pawel said.

Despite Gloria's objection Pawel continued to operate his *Gopher Hole Boutique* and shoot destructive birds and rodents but like his father, he would never harm a beaver, which Wildlife authorities said would soon become extinct.

For her part to deal with the eco system, Gloria, a frontline defender of the environment, risked her life when she walked onto the ice-covered Moose Lake on an early winter day in order to save a snowy owl. The bird was stranded for more than a day on the edge of the lake when Gloria and her father ventured out onto thin ice. They thought the owl, two=hundred feet from shore, had become frozen into the ice and would die. As they approached the bird it wasn't the case. The owl began hopping around vigorously, trying to get away but it couldn't fly. Gloria and her father finally circled the bird coming close enough to capture it by throwing a gunnysack over it.

"It just kept trying get away but it seems like its wing is broken. It kept hopping on the ice," Gloria said to the vet when she brought the bird to the Bonnyville Animal and Bird Hospital.

Gloria, who was quite a talker, was upset by the apparent indifference of Wildlife officers when she had requested help to rescue the bird, but was told that nature can be cruel and to leave the bird alone. Gloria, nor residents near Bonnyville, had ever seen a snowy owl before. The young bird was mostly white in color with black speckles and heavily feathered legs.

While examining the bird the vet said, "Snowy owls nest in the Arctic. They are daytime hunters and thrive in the north. At this time of the year however, the birds move south where there is more daylight."
The young bird had dislocated its wrist joint in the wing and was held in the veterinary shelter for a month before with Gloria's assistance, was turned loose.

Like Gloria, Roman too learned something about the eco system after Chief Dion showed him how to catch fish through an ice hole during winter. As with summer fishing, ice fishing is considered most successful at dawn and dusk. It was a balmy February evening on nearby Muriel Lake that Roman, accompanied by a dog dug a hole in the thick ice with an axe and a spade. (An auger wasn't invented yet) and sat on a bucket, fishing rod in one hand and a bottle of chokecherry wine in the other. While huddled around a small hole in the ice, waiting for the big one, Roman

suddenly had a rude wakening – a muskrat popped out of the hole with a sudden splash, and then back in, frightening him as he said to Evdokia later, "Like seeing a ghost."
Seeing the furry rodent Roman dropped his fishing rod and ran home, as if he was practicing for the Summer Olympics. Roman was so frightened that he nearly wet his pants, so instead he urinated on the ice and also forgot to mark the hole to protect a passerby accidentally spraining an ankle, or clean up after the dog.
When Roman arrived home and told Evdokia of the frightening experience she said to him, "Roman, maybe you had too much wine to drink?"
"No, I just opened the bottle when this happened."
"At any rate you should have marked the ice hole, not peed on the ice and picked up the dog doo doo."
"Why so?" Roman asked.
"Because that's where the Indians on the Kehewin Reserve, and the 'Big Shots' from Bonnyville who own cottages by the lake, get their drinking water."

"Okay, okay," I'll do what you say tomorrow when I'll try ice fishing again."

The following evening ice cubes were flying in every direction when Roman and Jacques were fishing side by side and Jacques accused Roman of catching more than his allowed limit of jackfish. In the excitement and not wanting to break a law, Roman threw his fish back into the ice hole, and when Gateau wasn't looking, did the same with his. Seeing what had happened Jacques hardly couldn't keep his toque on his head and was about to dump Roman into the same hole, but instead he puffed at his pipe three times, spat upon the ice, raised his arms in desperation and screamed, "What else can one expect from a Bohunk?"

When the weather warmed up so did the rivalry between Jacques and Roman. During summer Roman's Plymouth Rock chickens often crossed the road in search of food and enter Jacques's yard. Seeing the birds Jacques would pick up a slingshot, place a pebble in the elastic, aim and release it – zing, striking the fowl in a wing or a leg.

This made Roman terribly angry and to Evdokia in a retaliatory way said, "Our chickens will not lay grade `An` eggs if they are injured. I'm going to get even with the Frenchman."

The following afternoon, the chickens entered the Jacques's yard an umpteenth time, so Roman asked his son to retrieve the birds. Pawel chased and chased the chickens but came home with only eleven.
"That's okay, you did all right," Roman said, "We are missing only six. Don't worry; I'll get even with Monsieur Gateau soon."
"Why are you going to get even?" Pawel asked.
"Because, he's a bad peasuper."

# CHAPTER FIVE

When spring arrived in 1931 beavers stalked a creek that ran through the Gateau and Kowalchuk's properties causing havoc to nearby trees, plugging a culvert and flooding the creek all because of a dam the beavers had built. Roman spent two days hacking a channel through the sturdy dam, which was still frozen in the middle. The dam built on the Kowalchuk's property and on a sharp bend, had altered the course of the creek that began eroding an embankment back of the Gateau barn.

When it came to busting the beaver dam with an axe and a shovel, Roman may have won the battle but not the war – the tenacious nocturnal animals returned each night, and each time that they did, Roman returned in the morning to keep the channel clear, hoping the beavers finally got the message.

To protect large trees from the fur-bearing, tireless rodents, Roman wrapped the base of the trunks with wire mesh and when that didn't work and night came, he flashed lights and rang bells to get rid of the beavers but they always came back to build, to reinforce and to gather provisions. The beaver/Roman battle continued and was observed by Jacques who one night said to his wife, "The stupid Hunky refuses to shoot the beavers. If this continues much longer our barn will be flooded and so will the pigpen."

That night, Jacques sneaked to the Kowalchuk's property where the beavers were active and blew up the dam with several sticks of dynamite. Roman and Evdokia were sleeping at the time. Hearing the explosion they jumped to their feet, Roman put on his rubber boots and overalls, grabbed Evdokia by the arm and rushed to the beaver dam site. When they arrived and saw debris strewn all over, Roman crossed his arms over his chest and to Evdokia said, "I wonder what the *peasouper* will do next to aggravate us?"

That was not the last of the problems with the crappy neighbor because a week later, the Kowalchuk cat strolled over and crapped in Jacques flower garden. Jacques immediately called the Bonnyville Municipal Office to complain, but was told that there was no

municipal cat bylaw so felines were free to scratch and dig anywhere they wanted. Jacques wasn't a man Roman wanted to cross too often, so when he met Roman next day, he said to him, "Roman, I'm going to kill your cat next time it comes into my yard."
And purchased a silencer for his rifle.

Roman didn't believe Jacques would be so cruel as to kill a pretty feline but next time the cat was missing. Jacques burst out with laughter as the Kowalchuk family went up and down the road calling, Kitty, Kitty, Kitty." To no avail, there was no kitty cat. Finally Roman found enough courage to walk to the Gateau residence and ask Jacques, "Have you seen our cat?"
"Yes," Jacques replied.
"Where?"
"In the garbage can, dead."
That was not the end of infamy between Jacques and Roman, as Roman set his own trap in hopes of catching Jacque's cat and placed a sardine next to the entrance gate. As soon as Roman caught Jacques's cat, he took it to the Society for Animal Prevention of Cruelty to Animals, not to Bonnyville but

to Fort Kent, a hamlet ten miles east of Bonnyville on Highway 28.

Jacques didn't think of calling the Fort Kent SPCA for his missing cat. When the feline wasn't claimed, an elderly couple adopted it.

During the spring of 1931, the Kowalchuk farm had the appearance of a petting zoo. There were horses, cows, sheep, goats and a dog named Pushka, which could do back flips and retrieve a sock or a hat thrown a distance. Of course there were also cats, turkeys, pigs and chickens that included a Plymouth Rock hen named Koorka, which became a stepmother to five goslings.

Koorka was one of Kowalchuk's best layers and decided to hoard her eggs until she had a nest full and then hatch them. The Kowalchuk's were watching for such an event and bought five goose eggs from the Barba's and switched them for Koorka's own eggs, with the hope that she would hatch the goose eggs and take care of the goslings. The Kowalchuk's weren't disappointed.

Koorka accepted the larger eggs and continued the hatching process of keeping the eggs warm and turning them frequently.

The hen was checked daily knowing the most
critical time would come when the goslings
began to appear.

"Will Koorka accept the goslings?" Evdokia
asked Roman to which he took a step forward
and replied; "Only time will tell."


At last the eggshells began to crack and out
crawled five little green goslings. The
Kowalchuk's watched anxiously for Koorka's
reaction.

"Will Koorka abandon them?" Kwitka asked.
In response Roman said, Jacques Gateau may
even shoot them."

But the Kowalchuk's underestimated
Koorka's maternal instincts. They had no way
of knowing what went on in Koorka's mind
when she first saw her step-gosling.

Perhaps she was a first time mother and did
know what to expect. Maybe Koorka was
more sophisticated than the other hens and
simply put the blame of her babies' rooster for
supplying such queer genes.

In any event Koorka seemed to realize that as
a single parent, no matter how handicapped
the offspring's, it was her responsibility to

raise them, and she went about it in a way that some humans could emulate.

Koorka taught the goslings that a certain clucking call meant danger was near and they must rush to the shelter of her wings.

Koorka protected them from hawks, animals of prey, rain, sleet and anything else that might harm them. Her protective wings and warm body provided a haven from any form of discomfort and danger. In their daily feeding, if Koorka considered any food too hard for the goslings to digest, she crushed it in her beak, and then spat it out for the goslings to eat.

Baby goslings are adorable little creatures and are soft and cuddly to hold. When the Kowalchuk's spoke to them the goslings always answered in the happy sounding, "cheep, cheep, cheep," voices.

"No wonder Koorka loves them so much," Kwitka said.

But one day Koorka came rushing to Evdokia in a very agitated state flapping her wings and scratching the ground with her feet.

"What's the matter? Where are your babies?" Evdokia asked the animated hen.

After more cluck-cluck-clucking Koorka hurried to the creek that ran through the Kowalchuk and Gateau farms.

There Koorka and Evdokia found five little web-footed goslings enjoying a swim. This was beyond Koorka's comprehension. Apparently her cry of an alarm was overshadowed by a stronger call from the creek.

Using pieces of bread Evdokia gave Koorka a hand by coaxing the goslings out of the water. Koorka did not scold her children for their transgression and forgave them like any mother would, under her wings that night.

But the cuddly little goslings soon became bigger creatures and within several weeks grew one-half size of Koorka and no longer was there room under her wings but they seemed reluctant to give up as a family unit.

When night and bedtime came, the goslings put their heads under Koorka even if there was little room for them. Koorka slept the nights in a half-standing position, eyes closed and surrounded by five goslings' backs and tails sticking out.

But Koorka's and the goslings' relationship had to end, and it did, as it was time for the goslings to go on their own as they were growing into adulthood. Koorka's work as a parent had been done.

This happened when the goslings had a call from the creek a second time, and they went swimming not realizing what dangers faced them. As soon as the goslings crossed to Gateau's side of the farm he had them for his family Easter dinner.

The Kowalchuk's too enjoyed their Easter dinner but it did not have goose meat on the menu but among other goodies: pyrohy, holubtsi, cabbage rolls, beet borscht and paska. The feast Evdokia prepared with Kwitka's help would make any mother proud and included kapusta, kolbasa, a strawberry dessert and hard-boiled chicken eggs in a variety of colors.

Spinach water was used for a green-colored egg, raw beets for red, and onion skins for an orange-brown effect, vegetable dye or food coloring to dye eggs blue, purple and yellow. Strips of masking tape were used for geometric patterns on a colored background.

When the eggs were colored they were placed into a wicker basket and during mass on Saturday, when the Kowalchuk's picked up a bottle of holy water, were blessed by Father Joseph Lapointe

As for the kapusta and kolbasa the main ingredients were courage, sauerkraut and garlic sausage. The kapusta was in wooden barrel and included dill pickles, dilled green tomatoes and sour cabbage leaves. The kapusta was two-thirds full of shredded cabbage, crisp and white, the sausage in rolls and spiced with garlic and a smoky flavor. Kapusta and kolbasa are misunderstood but that's okay," Evdokia said to Kwitka.
"Why is that?" Kwita asked.

"Because most people in Canada use canned sauerkraut, which is salty, limpy and tasteless. Canned kraut has turned the English and French speaking into cabbage haters.
"So that is why kids at school call Ukrainians a cabbage head?"Kvita asked.
"It could be."

"But every time they call us a 'cabbage head' we in turn to them say, "I see London. I see France. I see your underpants."

In any event when the kapusta and kolbasa were done the combination was put into a cool place only to be warmed up on Easter Sunday.

To top off the Easter dinner, Roman brought several bottles of chokecherry wine from the cellar and proposed a toast to members of his family too, despite the difficult times, enjoy prosperity in their new homeland.

It was shortly after the Easter holidays that Evdokia received a letter from her sister in Ukraine. The letter in part read:

Dear Evdokia,

On January 5, 1930 the Communist Party as part of a five-year plan has started the machinery of Collectivization. The Russian peasantry is demonstrating little opposition to Moscow because of their past tradition of communal farming where the land is owned by the village and not an individual.

As you know Ukraine on the other hand has an independent, individualistic farming tradition of private ownership of land.

The Russian communal spirit is something foreign to the farmers of Ukraine and they are opposing it bitterly. One way is by slaughtering their livestock before joining, however, a death penalty has been passed for such action.

Opposition to Collectivization is only half of the story why Moscow is creating a famine in Ukraine. Watch and see there will be millions of us dead.
More in my next letter.
Filipa in Lvov (1931)

# CHAPTER SIX

In Canada consequences of the Depression and the ineptitude of government leaders in dealing with poverty hardened the determination of men and women to ensure that poverty would not strike again. On Citizenship Day in 1932 the Kowalchuk's renounced their Ukrainian nationality and became British Subjects, which among other benefits, gave adult immigrants the right to vote.

At the Court House in Bonnyville Roman and Evdokia, after sending Pawel and Kwitka to school, appeared at Citizenship Court where Magistrate Alphonse Mussault asked each candidate a question or two about Canada. Monsieur Mussault directed the first question to Roman which was, "Who are the king and queen of Canada?"

"King George V and his wife Mary," Roman replied.

"Correct," Magistrate Mussault said and turning to Evdokia asked, "As a British subject you have certain rights. Name two."

"To vote and to seek an elected office."

"Correct," Magistrate Mussault said again and then went on to other candidates seeking citizenship and pledged an oath of allegiance to their new homeland.

After twenty-one Ukrainians, Poles, Swedes and Italians answered similar questions, Magistrate Mussault congratulated each candidate and while shaking their hand, handed out certificates of citizenship and to each candidate said, "Congratulations. On behalf of the King and Queen of England it gives me great deal of pleasure to declare that you are now a British subject and a citizen of Canada."

Each candidate responded with, "Thank you, sir."

Their reaction varied. Some grinned broadly while others had tears in their eyes. Several bowed their heads while others like Roman and Evdokia, hugged each other. Afterwards the new British subjects lined up to have their picture taken with the Magistrate and a RCMP officer dressed in a red tunic, to receive their commemorative citizenship *Bible*.

When Pawel and Kwitka returned home from school that day they found their parents still dressed in their Sunday best
Roman and Evdokia were now officially British subjects and so were Pawel and Kwitka.

Overall it was a good spring but when early summer arrived the rains, which should have come, withheld themselves and during daytime there wasn't a cloud in the sky and at night the bright stars shone their cruel beauty. The soil in the field that Roman and Evdokia cultivated dried and cracked and the young wheat stalks which sprung up courageously with the coming of spring stopped growing and stood motionless for the cutworms, caterpillars and grasshoppers, to strip every blade of grass, grain and leaf that led many homesteaders to think that if the end of the world was coming to an end, the unwelcome insects were the first sign. It was not a case of a minnow swallowing a whale as topsoil blew away and grasshoppers were so thick they clogged radiators of cars, made roads slippery and even chewed clothing hanging on the clothes line.

Indeed Mother Nature wasn't kind to the Kowalchuk's, as chickens and turkeys gobbled up the hoppers by the hundreds, giving a vile taste to their flesh and eggs.

Never-the- less for seven days Roman and Evdokia thought of nothing but their land and like many homesteaders began to quote Scripture to justify their fears. This occurred when Evdokia said to Roman, "It's like in the *Bible* during the time of the Pharaoh and the Israelites. If we aren't freezing to death we are praying for rain."

And Evdokia may have been right with that assessment because for reasons unfathomable by prophets and long-time Bonnyville residents, conditions were similar to the Ten Plagues in the *Bible*.

There was no rain and the nearby slough dried into a cake of clay and the water in the well sank so low that Evdokia broke into a sob and to Roman said, "If we boil our food and have a bath the garden goes dry."

Lice and mosquitoes were prevalent. Pawel and Kwitka developed sores while walking to school barefooted. Next, a fire destroyed the chicken coup and a hailstorm that followed flattened the wheat field, which was left of it.

"What are we trying to prove?" Evdokia said, frustrated.

One disappointing month turned into two, two into three when during a cold winter day a piece of phlegm had lodged into Nicholas's throat, shutting the air from his lungs, and he eventually died. At first it seemed just a tiny cold such as children often have and quickly recover. When Evdokia got up in the morning she found Nicholas strangely cold and already blue.

Dr. Sabourin and Father Lapointe were summoned to the house and tried to comfort the Kowalchuk's family in their grief.

"Do not blame yourselves. The Lord giveth. The Lord takes away," Father Lapointe said. But all the soothing words of the priest brought no solace. Evdokia said her guilt was her own and only she could expunge it. Evdokia was sorry she had sent so much time helping Roman sawing wood and should have paid more attention to their infant son. When Nicholas died old country customs were followed. A family member stayed up with the casket all night and immediate members of the family wore black for a certain period of time.

 And if black clothing was not available (many times none were) a black arm band was used to signify that the family was in mourning. Evdokia had her hair covered with a kerchief (babushka).

It is necessary to have the right "papers," as well as Evdokia had made two crosses. The larger black and white cross was placed in the hands of the corps and smaller cross was placed around his neck. The papers were a strip printed like a crown which was placed on Nicholas's forehead and a prayer which was folded up and placed in his hands. The prayer, according to Roman and Evdokia, is a passport of sorts. The deceased must present it to Saint Peter in order to gain admission to heaven.

The mirrors in the home were covered with cloth to keep Nicholas's soul from looking at them and getting trapped. Clocks were stopped. A floral arrangement was made in the image of a clock to indicate the time of death.

Windows, doors and locks were opened for a short time, so the soul could get out of the house

The shroud was sewn without any knots (knots might tie up either the soul of the deceased or the affairs of the surviving family members). Roman spoke on behalf of his son, asking forgiveness of the Kowalchuk family for any wrong done to the child and child in turn saying farewell to the stove, home, barn and cattle.

When the body was taken from the house, the coffin was touched three times to the threshold, for the deceased to say goodbye to the home that he had lived in.

There was a period when family members were not allowed to go to the movies or to listen to the radio. This was out of respect for the dead.

The child had a simple funeral as Father Lapointe said mass in the St. Louis church in Bonnyville where the Kowalchuk family sat in the front pew, distraught.

During the mass Evdokia, wearing a black veil, often knelt and asked herself questions one of which was, "Why did Nicholas have to die?"

She even went as far as to believe God had taken her third child because she tried to shoot a deer at time, like the Kowalchuk family, was short of food.

As soon as the mass was over, Nicholas's body was taken to a downtown cemetery for burial where tombstones had mostly French names: Filion, Mercier, Lambert, Ouimet and Rondeau among others. There were only a handful of Anglo Saxon names on graves because most of the English-speaking around Bonnyville were Protestants, and Protestants had their own cemetery.

Next day, Roman and Evdokia rose at dawn, fed the animals and then made a cross from two pieces of birch wood. After having breakfast, and Pawel and Kwitka had gone to school, Roman and Evdokia climbed into a cutter pulled by a horse, and drove to the cemetery where infant Nicholas was buried. It was a sunny morning but even at 11:00 a. m. it was cool.

Neither Roman nor Evdokia spoke as they slowly placed the cross on Nicholas's grave. It was the most difficult work they had done and by far the most important. Both began to cry and soon the soil that covered the grave became saturated with tears.

The cross and the tears were a symbol of difficult times the Kowalchuk family, and immigrants like them, were experiencing in their adopted land.

After the cross was placed, Roman took Evdokia's hand and softly said, "I must say Providence was kind enough to leave us with two healthy children. We'll do our best to educate Pawel and Kwitka. Hope and pray that they achieve their goals in life that they have set for themselves. As for Nicholas's grave we'll place a headstone out of marble as soon as we are able too."

That evening, after the chores had been done, other Ukrainian families arrived to mourn at Kowalchuk home and together recited prayers. Once the praying was done, a light lunch was served and Kwitka sang a song that she learned from a cylinder record her father had purchased at an auction sale – *Ave Maria*.

Her performance led one mourner to request an encore while another said, "Kwitka, yours is a voice one hears in a hundred years."

Kwitka had a knack of making small events startling. Besides her other assets Kwitka's singing voice gave the song more meaning than there was in words.
Although Kwitka was no *Marian Anderson* everyone seemed to enjoy her singing.

For the next several months Roman and Evdokia struggled through the motions of existence, grieving. Angry at the world, angry with themselves, angry at one another, they raged, Roman in silence, Evdokia in words. But slowly at first then gaining momentum, Roman and Evdokia healed themselves and were healed by others. Most important of all however, Evdokia forgave herself that it was her fault Nicholas had died.

As soon as the first pussy willow buds disappeared and the month of May arrived, the Kowalchuk's planted a garden, purchased a seed drill from an implement dealer and planted fifty acres into wheat that would ripen in three months.

Both the garden and the wheat flourished compared to the year before, although there were patches of wild oats, Canada and south thistles, and quack grass in one corner of the field.

When summer arrived the Kowalchuk's again picked wild berries and bartered them for necessities

The biggest profit this time however, came not from the berries but from digging for the native Seneca roots used in cold remedy medicines.

Once the roots were dried in the sun they were packed into gunnysacks and delivered to the Royal Chinese Restaurant where Lee Wong acted as an agent for a Chinese herbal company.

It was at the restaurant that farmers of all stripes met and over a cup of coffee or tea and complained about the weather, the government and the debts each incurred.

Aside from operating a restaurant business Lee Wong practiced in his residence above the restaurant, *ear coning*. Ear coning primarily is an ancient Chinese home remedy for cleaning and removing excess wax and debris from one's ear.

The middle aged Wong would lay a client on a bed and then insert a hollow candle in to his or her ear. He then lit he candle, and as it slowly burned, a vacuum was created that dislodged and drew out the superfluous and debris, which as a rule in a farmer's ear there was plenty of.

According to Wong not only did coning remove wax and dirt from the ears but also detoxifies the sinuses and lymph, improves one's hearing and alleviates snoring. For a one-dollar fee, having one's ear coned was considered a good deal.

"Buying Seneca roots for curing a cold and ear coning will compensate for any losses incurred should my restaurant be foreclosed," Wong said.

# CHAPTER SEVEN

It was in 1933 that Kowalchuck family met its obligation to the government of Canada in 1933 by having their homestead fenced, shelter built, and land broken and seeded into grain. On the day the inspector came for the final inspection, he was so impressed with the progress made that a clear title to the property was given within a week. The list of improvements included:

An 18 X 26 log house at a value of $150

A 20 X 26 log barn valued at $50

A 14 X 16 granary valued at $20

A chicken coop valued at $15

Two miles of fencing valued at $30

Fifty-five acres of land was broken thirty of which was cropped

Seven head of cattle and two horses were maintained

In a sworn statement, Nick Barba and Chief Dion, verified accuracy of the improvements.

As soon as the title was registered, Roman went to a bank and borrowed enough money to buy another quarter-section of land.
And not only extra land but also a used red Ford pickup truck that had 150,000 miles on the odometer, and a cream separator that separated the cream from the milk. This done Roman said to Evdokia, "The farm is mortgaged to the hilt and the little cash we have covers only the interest."
While other farmers were vocal in their envy about the pickup purchased, there was
A bone of contention between Roman and Evdokia on how they were going to pay for it at a time when gasoline and insurance prices were high and other farmers had been foreclosed on theirs. But Roman felt a certain amount of debt was necessary if one was to succeed in farming.

Now that the Kowalchuk's had three-hundred and twenty acres of land, this enabled them to grow more wheat and potatoes and graze more cattle that increased to ten cows, a bull and eight calves. Roman would have had ten calves but farmers in the area were losing livestock to predators.

But marauding coyotes met their match when the Kowalchuk's lost the two calves within a week. On each occasion the coyotes came right up to the pasture and took away the newborn.

"So it is causing quite a problem," Roman said to Pawel and the father and son, held an all-day/night marksmanship workshop in shooting as they tried to bring the burgeoning coyote population under control.

As the Kowalchuk's were waiting for a coyote to appear during daytime, they spotted not a badger or a porcupine but a skunk strutting across the yard. Seeing the animal the dog, Pushka, chased it, but the inevitable happened – she got sprayed.

"What an awful smell!" Kwitka said holding on to her nose tightly.

Everyone including Roman seemed to agree there was a pungent odor so Evdokia as soon as the skunk ambled away suggested the dog needed a bath immediately.

"I'll give her a bath if you show me how," Kwitka said.

First you need tomato juice."

"Tomato juice?"

"If not tomato juice one can use your father's chokecherry wine."

"Tomato juice or wine to deodorize a skunk?

"You can use either but make certain you don't let the dog inside the house until the odor his gone.``

"Okay, I'll use some of Dad's chokecherry wine but please tell me, how will the wine get rid of the smell?"

In jest Evdokia smilingly said, "Not only will the wine get rid of the smell but also get the fleas," when she was interrupted by Pawel who said, "I think you are making this up?"

"Evdokia's reply was, "This is what will happen. The fleas will get drunk on the wine they drink and start throwing rocks at each other. Watch, there will be so much commotion that the odor will disappear and the fleas will kill themselves."

In the end it involved wresting Pushka into a back yard tub, shampoo and water. The one-hour ordeal could have been better spent listening to the birds singing than putting an arm lock on a wet dog. For this the dog was given a small piece of meat to enjoy.

Although there were no coyotes seen in the area, there was a magpie attempting to take a small piece of meat away from Pushka that had been given a bath minutes earlier.

Again the Kowalchuk's watched as the black and white bird attempted to take a small piece way from the dog.
At first the magpie sat on a nearby fence and then landed four feet of the dog, teasing her. Eventually the magpie soft talked Pushka to give up the meat with its constant, "Yak, Yak, Yak."
Pushka moved only slightly and after several minutes of grandstanding the magpie pecked the dog on the tail. Pushka let out a bark and while turning around, the magpie picked up the meat and flew away.

As for the cream separator Roman had purchased, it was placed in the kitchen where it separated the cream from the milk each morning and evening. As part of their chores Pawel and Kwitka gave a helping hand in milking the cows, carrying out the swill and feeding the hogs.

They also carried in the firewood to feed the kitchen stove and space heater that kept the house warm.

While Pawel and Kwitka did their chores Evdokia washed clothes on a washboard using homemade soap that was made from boiled fat and lye molded into squares.

On a farm no matter how careful one could be about taking off rubber boots and overalls, the mud seemed to drift in all directions.

Mud was the least of it. There was also cow manure that was used to fertilize the garden. For drying, an outside clothesline was the answer. A wooden floor throughout the home was scrubbed on bended knees. With two active children they were scrubbed often.

By now, cream was delivered to the creamery in Bonnyville in a variety of containers ranging from ten-gallon cream cans to five-pound lard pails. One sunny afternoon after delivering the cream to the creamery and receiving a cheque, Roman said to Evdokia, "It's time we place a proper tombstone on Nicholas's grave."

"Let's do it, order one," Evdokia replied and Roman did, through an Alberta Monument catalogue in Edmonton.

When the tombstone arrived in Bonnyville, Roman and Evdokia drove in a wagon to the Canadian National Railway station to pick it up. Then they drove to the cemetery that was acrid as a desert, flowers on graves wilted and only the sound on that hot day was the chirping of grasshoppers as they jumped from one grave to another.

There were no trees and grass growing between plots was scorched to a point that if one dropped a cigarette or a match, the entire burial ground could become an inferno. When they reached Nicholas's grave site Roman and Evdokia were dismayed. They could not believe that such a thing could happen in Canada.
The tiny wooden cross marking the child's grave was smashed into splinters and the soil covering the casket was emblazoned with spray painted six-inch letters *A BABY HUNKY LIES BURIED HERE.*

Referring to the wooden cross, Evdokia said, "A complete smashup. A drunk must have done it?"

Saddened, Roman replied, "No drunk would stoop that low."

"Who do you think did it?"

"Someone who isn't Ukrainian."

It didn't take long for Roman and Evdokia to remove the tiny pieces of the wooden cross and replace it with a marble one. The words read simply:

**NICHOLAS KOWALCHUK**
**1929 – 1932**

No Longer In Our Hearts to Share
But In Our Hearts You'll Always Be There
Roman, Evdokia, Pawel and Kwitka
Kowalchuk

Besides selling cream and cattle, the Kowalchuk's raised hogs and brought them to market as soon as they weighed two-hundred and ten pounds. That same winter, when the moon was at first quarter, Roman slaughtered a hog for the family. After he shot and bled the hog, Roman dipped the carcass into a barrel of boiling water underneath a tripod made of timber.

With a sharp knife he removed the hair and sliced the animal through the middle from the head towards the tail, and let out the intestines.

Besides the meat ordinarily used he saved the pig's head, feet, heart, liver, kidneys and the bladder that Roman gave to Pawel who rolled it in ashes and as soon as the fat was removed put in several peas inside, blew it up and tied the end with a piece of string.

Once this was done Pawel used the bladder as a punching bag. Unfortunately with the first hard punch, it busted.

From that day onward Pawel begged his father to buy him a real punching bag and a pair of boxing gloves. Roman said he would as soon as he was able too, provided Josiah Alexander gave him lessons and Pawel in turn, pass on what he learned to his sons who weren't born yet.

Both agreed.

With unemployment everywhere Roman had ample time to think how to overcome poverty. He had heard on the radio that during Prohibition, a hotel owner in Saskatchewan by the name of Sam Bronfman began an empire with a bootlegging operation across the Saskatchewan border into United States. Roman on subsequent radio programs also heard that Samuel Bonfman in the province of Saskatchewan funded the Liberal party, desperate to become the first Jew in Canada's senate. The Liberals were happy to take his money, but were afraid to make the Senate appointment, because of Bronfman's bootleg background.

"If Bronfman can do it, why can't I on a smaller scale," Roman rationalized. "Look at Bronfman, he's now Canada's Big Shot."

The temptation to emulate Bronfman was there but after debating bootlegging with himself. Roman was afraid that if he ever got caught by the RCMP he would be deported to Ukraine.

"Heaven forbid," Roman said to himself. "Sure hard times are here but they aren't that difficult that my family has nothing to eat and I should take the risk to be deported. Under Stalin's rule, where a forced famine is taking place that would be unthinkable."

The Kowalchuk's listened to the radio daily.

There was the *Ukrainian Hour*, which taught Ukrainians how to speak English and played Ukrainian music. There were hourly newscasts, interviews with prominent people and Wilf Carter singing songs like *Beautiful Yoho Valley.* Foster Hewitt shouted, "He shoots! He scores!" describing National Hockey League games. There was also the World Series, boxing championships and the most popular program of all, *Back to the Bible* each Sunday with William Aberhart and his student, Ernest Manning.

# CHAPTER EIGHT

The effects of the Depression during 1934 were not the same across the country. The people most severely affected were those engaged in the primary industry and those out of work. The average income of most people fell but in Alberta it fell drastically. When Roman first came to Canada the yearly income was $500. Four years later it was down to $150. This was intensified by a series of crop failures and draughts. Two thirds of the population of Alberta were destitute and on relief.  These were desperate times. The Kowalchuk's and thousands like them were desperate people.

Evdokia in a letter to her sister, Filipa, in Ukraine, described life in Alberta this way:

Dear Filipa,

"Thank you for your letter. But I must tell you we are now in debt and can't afford to pay the bank a loan we took out for an additional quarter of land, a pickup truck and a cream separator.

Several of our cows have died for lack of hay. Our meat now consists of fish and wild animals and birds that Roman shoots.
The brown bread is course and we are out of sugar, coffee and flour. There is little fruit to enjoy, as no longer are there wild berries but plenty of vegetables. Thank God chickens keep laying eggs and we have plenty rolled oats to eat. I'm not certain which is worse, living in Ukraine or Canada."
Sister Evdokia – Bonnyville, Alberta, Canada (1934)

Pawel, listening to his mother said, "Yeah, Mom, you should have also told her we have rolled oats for breakfast, lard sandwiches, hard boiled eggs that smell like sulpher, for lunch at school."
"Isn't that the truth?" Kwitka agreed. "And the French kids at school laugh at us. Gloria and Marcel Gateau at least have peanut butter sandwiches."
In response Evdokia said, "Don't remind me. Why the Gateau children have peanut butter sandwiches for lunch is because their parents are enjoying the benefit of a government relief."

"Then why aren't we on relief too?"
Evdokia put her head between her hands.
"Your father has applied."
"And what happened?"Pawel asked.
"The municipal secretary, who is French
Canadian, Mr. Laporte, said if we applied for
relief he would personally ask the government
to deport us to the Old Country." Evdokia
said.

"I don't understand why the government
would want to do that especially now that we
are British subjects."
"Neither do we. It seems that those who are
running the municipality don't want to see
one of different heritage, especially a Slav, to
infringe on their territory."
This was a time too that hungry single men
worked for the federal government improving
the National Park System in Relief Camps.
Work usually lasted two months, the pay
$5.00 a month. The food at these camps was
wholesome compared to what alien internees,
including Pawlo Biely and Petro Czorny
endured during their interment at the
Brandon, Manitoba Concentration Camp
during the First World War.

Human misery and social dislocation was taking place.

For unemployed men in labor camps, life was dreary and a succession of days in which there was little to do but lineup for soup, while enforced idleness corroded all sense of human dignity. For others, it was a series of unsuccessful attempts to earn a dime or two doing almost anything. *Brother Can You Spare a Dime?* And *Hallelujah I'm a Bum* where popular songs, only this time they were played on the radio. Kwitka learned to sing the tunes as well.

As time went on, Roman joined a group of men and traveled back and forth across Western Canada on and in freight cars in search of work.

While in Calgary he attempted to see his friend William Aberhart, but was harassed by railway police, driven from the city by local police and told to go home. In the process, when Roman did return, he said to his family, "I was treated like a parasite."

Another time, Roman joined two-hundred men on a treck to Ottawa to meet Prime Minister Bennett but Bennett flatly refused to meet the delegates.

The unemployed came en mass to the capital and Bennett eventually did agree to talk to their spokesman but only after the prime minister arranged an armored car and extra police to be on hand.

The prime minister felt he was doing his best in fulfilling promises he had made and was led to believe there were forces at work, which in attacking him, was attacking law and order. What else could be fighting for the rights of workers but Communism? And Communism meant revolution.

# CHAPTER NINE

During 1934 Aberhart introduced Major C. H. Douglas's *Social Credit* on his *Back to the Bible* program in Alberta. Douglas, an engineer in England and believed there was too much waste and under-industrialization. He believed there was insufficient purchasing power in the economy to fully use productive capacity. Douglas also advocated the government distribute money to restore the balance. To illustrate this point Douglas propounded the A plus B Therom, in which a represented wages paid to employees and B the overhead cost of production. Aberhart picked up the theme on his radio program and the religion he taught was *Bible* philosophy. Not only was the scripture taken as literal truth but certain passages, in particular the *Book of Revelation*, were treated as accurate predictions of coming events. The predictions appealed to Roman and Evdokia and many other people too.

Each Sunday after they had attended their own church, service  the Kowalchuk family sat near the radio and listened to *Back to the Bible* program, not for spiritual value but because Aberhart's dynamic personality. Aberhart had little difficulty in convincing followers of the rightness of his views as the Depression hit Alberta with a vengeance. The party in power, United Farmers of Alberta, wrestled with the problem but like R. B. Bennett's Conservative government in Ottawa did little, which put people back to work.

"Let's go and see Abe Goldman at the General Store," Evdokia suggested one day. "Remember he offered us a line of credit."

"An excellent idea. Whatever we do, we won't go on relief," Roman agreed and hitched a horse to a *Bennett* buggy(a term used in Canada during the Great Depression to describe a car which had its engine and windows taken out and was pulled by a horse – In the United states it was the Hoover Wagon) and with Evdokia by his side drove to town.

After tying the horse to a hitching post the couple walked along Main Street where they first stopped to see Lee Wong if the price of Seneca roots went up or down.

But when they reached the Royal Chinese Restaurant they were surprised to find a sign stapled on the front door that read *Temporarily Out Of Business*.

And when they reached Goldman's General Store, it too had a sign posted on the door but it read *Moved to San Francisco.*

Goldman started his Bonnyville business with merchandise acquired on credit. His lack of capital, the language barrier, perhaps even his strange appearance, made it impossible to compete with the Brosseau, Vallee and Kowalsky stores. This was particularly true because Goldman observed Sabbath on Saturday, a time when farmers and lumberjacks come to town to do their shopping.

Rumors persisted however, that why Goldman moved to California was not because of its climate but because he had found a sweetheart and didn't want anyone in Bonnyville know it.

Bankruptcies and foreclosures were getting to be common and it wasn't a surprise when a sheriff appeared at the Kowalchuk home and asked for a "Mr. Kowalchuk."

"That's me," Roman identified himself so the sheriff continued, "Mr. Kowalchuk, the bank where you obtained your loan says you are three months in arrears with your payments. When you bought the land, pickup and a cream separator you signed an agreement that would make payments faithfully.

Since you are unable to meet your commitment the bank is laying claim to your land and the machinery you purchased. A matter of fact the bank already has an offer on your property."

Surprised, Roman said, "The offer, who is it from?"

"His name is Jacques Gateau."

"I'll tear him from limb to limb the next time I see him. Please, ask the bank for a month extension."

Roman had heard on the radio that farmers and small businesses in Alberta were organizing themselves so he was more brave than usual and said, "If the bank doesn't grant me an extension there will be a high noon at our place when you return tomorrow."

The sheriff said he would relay the message to the bank but did not commit himself that one would be granted.

As soon as the sheriff left, Evdokia said, "This is more than I can stand. I'm going to have a nervous breakdown if this continues, the strain is so great."

When the sheriff returned the following day, Roman had set up a barricade in front of his gate. Eyeing the barricade the sheriff said, "The bank has agreed to give you a one-month extension. For only one month, that's it.

The bank says farming is a free enterprise. You go into it understanding the chances you take. You either make it or you don't."

Roman appreciated the extension and stayed up all night thinking about the debt and how to get rid of it. He was delighted too that Pawel and Kwitka had reached a level of education that they were skipping grades at Palm school and soon would be attending Bonnyville High School.

The following day, without members of the family knowing it, Roman was wracking his brain but not in vain, when he thought that *Horeewka* (home brew) was an integral part of Ukrainian culture.

It for instance was consumed in large quantities at country dances and Ukrainian weddings, which tradionally lasted several days.

Producing alcohol was certainly a source of extra income for farmers and much of the money was ploughed back into the farm, modern machinery. Larger homes and purchasing additional land.

Over a cup of coffee Roman said to himself, "Aha, I have a plan."

Next day he drove into town where he purchased copper tubing and several large crocks. When he returned to the farm, in the most forested area, he built a still, added a mash of wheat or potato, added yeast and the ingredients began brewing.

The homebrew Roman made was distilled alcohol of a powerful variety. Three parts of water were added to each part of alcohol to give it the approximate potency of government approved whiskey. This done, Roman sat on a stump and recalled what the sheriff had said about the bank loan, 'You get into it understanding you take chances.'

"Well, I'm going to take the risk and bootleg homebrew.

Evdokia and I should be out of debt by the time the foreclosure notice expires. If caught the fine is $100. Hopefully the RCMP won't find out."

Roman was playing the percentages and the plan worked. He kept the still and bootlegged his alcohol at country dances and weddings eventually selling enough moonshine enabling him to make a substantional bank payment.

He even came home with groceries and clothing for the family that wasn't accustomed to having. Roman also bought Pawel a pair of boxing gloves, Kwitka a guitar and a harmonica plus the latest edition of *Photoplay*, a Hollywood gossip magazine. For Evdokia, Roman purchased a second-hand piano.

When questioned about the sudden affluence Roman replied, "The money is due to the high grade of cream we sell to the creamery but Evdokia didn't believe him and her suspicion was confirmed, when two RCMP officers appeared at the homestead at a time Roman and Evdokia were visiting the Barbra's, and Pawel was home alone studying for a history exam.

The policemen searched the attic and then the cellar but found only chokecherry wine, which Roman had vinted. Seeing the two cops Pawel said to one, "I think there are several gallons of moonshine hidden in a manure pile behind the barn."

"Thank you for the tip," the first officer said and then Pawel watched for an hour as the cop and his partner dug through a pile of manure but didn't find any moonshine. When the policemen were leaving Pawel overheard one say, "That's okay, we'll catch the Hunky next time."

As soon as Roman and Evdokia returned home, Pawel told them about the policemen search.

Roman confessed that he had been bootlegging and received a severe reprimand from his wife and children.

Evdokia said, "Roman, you are breaking the law and must stop selling illegal booze as of right now."

"Or else you'll end up in jail," Pawel said.

"I know, I know. I just thought…"

"Thought what?" Evdokia interrupted.

Roman felt that if Bronfman could make a fortune bootlegging that perhaps he could do the same but on a smaller scale.

"I had to do something to pay off the bank and get us out of debt."

"Promise me one thing," Evdokia said.

"I'm listening,"

"As much as I enjoy playing the piano, that you dismantle the still and stop bootlegging. Do you understand what I'm saying?"

"I do," Roman replied, and did stop, but not until he paid off the entire bank loan and RCMP officers appeared on the Kowalchuk farm in another moonshine raid.

It was a day later, that Roman had another run-in with Jacques. Three cows belonging to Roman broke through a fence and entered

Gateau's wheat field that had already been threshed. Seeing the stray animals Jacques climbed on a horse and drove them to the nearest Pound where the animals were kept overnight.

In order to retrieve the cows Roman had to pay a $15 fine and promise to keep his cattle fenced inside his own property. The notice by the Pound Keeper was given on October 30 but the following day farmers were fall plowing and front yards were decorated with Halloween pumpkins.

After retrieving the cow's home, Roman was fed up with his out toilet outhouse knocked over each Halloween so he and Evdokia moved it to the edge of the six-foot deep hole. When darkness camel, Roman waited, hoping Jacques would come trick or treating and knock it over like he did the year before.

It wasn't Jacques who showed up however, but two teenage boys who took a run at the privy in hopes of knocking it down, but to no avail, the boys fell into the six foot deep hole, as Roman put it succinctly later that was, "Filled with shit."

The teenagers were identified as Marcel Mercier and Rene Lambert, two neighborhood teenagers Roman would have to deal with later.

Soon another Christmas arrived and Roman helped to build a Christmas concert stage at Palm school while Evdokia made the stage curtains out of bed sheets that were made out of flour sacks. Two weeks before concert time Roman chopped down a Christmas tree on the homestead and with Pawel and Kwitka's help delivered to the school in a sleigh pulled by a team of horses. As they drove along Pawel and Kwitka sang *Jingle Bells* and carols. At the school students decorated the tree with multi-colored bells, candy canes and tinsel.

On the way back home, Pawel and Kwitka were bundled up again in the sleigh with impatient horses chaffing at the bit. It was a three and one-half mile trip on a frosty moonlit night with only the sound of horses' hooves echoing in the snow and the jingling of their harness and bells, and now and again the far-off haunting sound of the nocturnal owl and the howling coyotes.

As the trip progressed Pawel and Kwitka gazed up at the clear sky and watched the full moon, the multi colored northern lights and shooting stars hit the horizon.

The following Friday, the Christmas concert was held in the evening. As Parents' Roman and Evdokia enjoyed the pantomimes, recitations, one-act plays and carol singing which Pawel and Kwitka participated in.
 Pawel who was master of ceremonies also read part of a speech former Prime Minister, John A. MacDonald, had made in the House of Commons. Kwitka recited *The Night before Christmas* and later in the concert did a song and dance routine, which had the audience burst out with laughter.

Following the concert, Josiah Alexander, who had children attending the same school, with a little makeup to cover his dark skin, played the role of Santa Claus and treated the students and pre-school children to a paper bagful of candy, nuts, apples and oranges. And then Alexander distributed gifts among the students who drew names.

Gloria had to buy a gift for Pawel and Kwitka for Walter Barba, a boy she didn't particularly like but his mother insisted one day would be her husband.

The girls and boys unwrapped their gifts. Pawel received a book about Canadian history and Kwitka a comb/looking glass set. Together the students gave Miss Cameron a set of pearl earrings.

Despite what appeared to be a joyous Christmas party, French and Anglo parents continued to speak of Slavs as *Hunkies* and some even propagandized against the existing immigration policy of the Canadian government, which focused on European countries.

Xenophobes feared that Ukrainians in particular, would lower their standard of living and that they themselves would become minorities.

This fear was most rampant by those who practiced a Protestant faith and were irritated when Catholic youngsters would say, "Catholic, Catholic ring the bell. Protestant, Protestant, go to hell."

As time marched on however, Ukrainian customs, food and songs, were adapting into Canadian way of life. Many Ukrainians learned to speak English or French fluently and to engage themselves in teaching and politics. By now Pawel and Kwitka were transferred from the country Palm school to the Bonnyville High School, which admitted students from grades nine to twelve. During this period in time CCF's national convention was held in Regina and the political party adopted a program known as the Regina 14-point Manifesto that dealt with socialization, external trade, freedom and social justice.

Despite of the appeal of the movement to many of his farming friends, Roman was a free enterpriser and became an enthusiast of William Aberhat's Social Credit Party. It was near the end of 1934 that Evdokia received a letter from her sister who lived in the community of Lvov. The disturbing letter in part read:

Dear Evdokia,

There are millions of victims in Ukraine of a man-made famine orchestrated by Dictator Josef Stalin of the USSR or whatever Russia calls itself.

It is considered the largest famine of the 20<sup>th</sup> century and a horrible act of genocide by hunger.

Under Soviet control, large quantities of wheat grown in Ukraine have been shipped to Russia last year leaving little for Ukrainians to eat. Many Ukrainians are hostile to the Soviet government, especially farmers in the fertile wheat-growing region. Many believe it's a deliberate policy to starve Ukrainians into submission. More in my next letter.

Filipa in Lvov (1934)

# CHAPTER TEN

While Pastor Aberhart was evangelizing
Alberta with religion and politics in 1935, he
stopped in Bonnyville where he renewed
friendship with the Kowalchuk family and
spoke to Pawel that seemed like an
extraordinary length of time. At the
Bonnyville High School gymnasium that
evening there was an overflow crowd of
farmers, lumberjacks and small businessmen,
many came as far as fifty miles to attend. At
the meeting Aberhart expounded about Social
Credit and quoted the *Book of Revelation*
from the *Bible.*

 But 1935 didn't begin well for the
Kowalchuk's, aside from Pawel and Kwitka
passing their grades with high marks at the
Bonnyville High School, which was run by
the Sisters of Assumption order of nuns.
Sister Mary Raphael was the principal and Ed
Ami, a lay vice-principal whose main purpose
was to teach French and to use the strap if
necessary.

While in High School Pawel, one of the
quietest and even tempered boys in class took
up debating and surprised everyone when he
wrote an essay titled *Why I Love Canada.*
Principal Raphael after reviewing it said,
"Pawel, that's excellent, when you finish
High School you must go on to University
and study Canadian history."
Kwitka on the other hand snorted, "You got to
be kidding?" but knew how to wrap her father
around her finger.
After each `A` she got on her report card
Roman would buy her a record for her
collection that now seemed a mile high.
Among the records Roman purchased that
year were: *All I Do Is Dream about You, Isle
of Capri, Winter Wonderland, Tumbling
Tumbleweeds* and *P. S. I Love You.*

It was an extremely dry spring and summer
and as hot as Hades and as soon as the school
holidays began in July, Bonnyville without a
warning, experienced a storm with thunder
and lightning, followed by hail the size of golf
balls, which destroyed most of the crops and
Pawel's stuffed souvenir gophers. Bonnyville

had summer storms before but none like this one.

It began at 5:00 p. m. when dark clouds appeared in the sky. Seeing the clouds approaching, Evdokia said to Roman, "Here we go again; watch as our poultry and animals may get killed."

Evdokia was correct with her prediction because the storm was so vicious that when it stopped Roman, found a dead calf that failed to find shelter in the pasture.

"I can't take this much longer, it can't go on forever," Evdokia complained. "Hail, snow, frost, wind, draught. In fifteen minutes we lose everything. When will it all end? Surely there must be a better place to farm in Canada than near Bonnyville. How about Saskatchewan? There are farms there that stretch as far as one can see."

Roman met each disaster with unshakeable faith so he said, "But Saskatchewan is subject to periods of draught also and the winters are just as cold as they are in Bonnyville."

"How about British Columbia? An orchard acreage, in the Okanagan Valley would suit me."

"Evdokia," Roman said, "I understand your disappointment and the strain mounting day by day. The radio says one-half million people are out of work in Canada and one of the best farmers in Bonnyville, William Brennan, says his farm will yield only 400 bushels instead of the normal four-thousand."

"So let's move to somewhere that has a moderate climate. I hear on *Back to the Bible*, from letters Aberhart receives, Penticton in British Columbia has two pristine lakes and a good and a safe place to raise a family."

"In British Columbia conditions aren't better," Roman replied while picking up a copy of the *Nouvelle* weekly newspaper. "Look. Factories are closing by the thousands and people are out of work. Many are in debt. No matter where one lives these are difficult times but we'll survive in Bonnyville."

At this point Roman had thoughts of making moonshine again but remembered the commitment he made to his family and decided to limit his expertise this time to making only chokecherry wine.

Although a severe hailstorm caused a lot of damage during the spring, a prairie fire that swept the Kowalchuk homestead during early autumn didn't. A fire had already consumed several acres of stubble after a passing motorist errantly tossed a cigarette to ignite it. The fire was well underway before Roman had noticed it as the stubble, grass, trees, and shrubs crackled for lack of moisture. Soon, more acres of stubble where wheat, barley, oats and alfalfa crops stood earlier, and a forest grove stood were consumed in minutes by the raging flames.

The ensuing fire, as it headed towards the fireguard guarding the house and barn, was pushed by a gusty wind with speeds of fifty miles an hour Seeing a huge black plume of smoke high in the sky Nick Barba, adjacent to the farm and Chief Dion from the near the Kehewin Indian Reserve, rushed to the scene to help. So did Jacques Gateau but he didn't stay long. While the fire was still a distance away and animals and fowl scattered in front, Roman and Evdokia made the rounds of the house to make certain Pawel and Kwitka were safe, then the yard and barn and where near a pile of hay Roman said, "Hang on!" And hitched a plow to his team of horses and plowed a wider fireguard as the flames were racing towards it. Roman, Barba and Dion then started back firing. The backfire was set along the edge of the fireguard. Having to burn against the wind it did not burn as fast as the wind-driven one and much easier to control. If the flames began to blow across the fireguard Evdokia threw buckets of water, which was drawn from the nearby creek in cans full. Chief Dion did not help carry any cans however, instead kneeled to the ground and after praying to the Great Spirit said, "You don't have much time once a fire starts. There's always the wind and it comes fast." "And the fireguard is all we have to depend on," Barba said after he had advised Roman earlier in the year not to overburden the soil by planting continuous heavy crops but to rotate and to be patient.

As soon as the three men with calloused hands, burnt one small strip of stubble, they started another and then another, while the wind was still vicious.

Great Spirit must have answered Chief Dion's prayer because several hours later there was a downpour, the backfire and the original, finally met and fire burnt itself out.

Some people continued to fight prairie fires in the municipality, others like Roman preferred scouring his homesteads burnt area because he felt fire was a natural part of the east central Alberta eco system and a burnt out forest is, suitable for more than cutting firewood and salvage logging.

Along with the two storms causing a lot of damage there was satisfaction too. It proved that Roman and Evdokia were equal to danger as well as to their partnership. They were proud the way they handled the storms, the fire and proud of each other.

It was during the month of October, that Pawel took a bottle of the wine to the annual Bonnyville Halloween High School Sadie Hawkins dance. Pawel was now 17 years of age and despite his initial language barrier was in grade twelve and Kwitka in grade eleven.

Roman drove Pawel and Kwitka to the dance
in his red pickup with instructions that he
would pick them up at midnight when the
dance was scheduled to end.
On his way home Roman was stopped at a
roadblock set up by the RCMP.

The roadblock was situated after Roman had
driven through a straight stretch of gravel
road and then a sharp curve. Not only were
two RCMP constables searching for
moonshine that evening but at the same time
if farmers were using *purple* gasoline in
vehicles, which they weren't allowed. When
the pickup came to a stop Roman opened the
door and stepped out. Before the door was
closed the taller cop asked, "Have you any
booze?"
"Definitely not, sir." Roman answered.
The two constables searched the pickup and
didn't find any but they did find that Roman
used purple gas in his vehicle.
"You have a choice, appear before magistrate
Alphonse Mussault or pay a fine of thirty
Dollars," one of the cops said.

Roman was relieved that the fine was only that amount and he had thirty days to pay it. "I'll pay the fine."

The feeling of relief lasted only seconds because as the policemen concluded their investigation one said to the other, "Those Hunkies work sixteen hours a day, if they work. Now they think they own the country. Most of them can't speak or write English. People like that should be deported to from where they came from."

At the Sadie Hawkins dance that night, Pawel and Gloria Gateau were inseparable and when Kwitka was asked by the master of ceremonies to "Sing several songs."
She did and then Pawel and Gloria slipped out of the gymnasium for a drink of chokecherry wine that Pawel had hidden on a nearby grassy lot.

As Pawel and Gloria sat they exchanged kisses while the bottle went back and forth. At the same time they engaged in a conversation that ranged about Gloria's concern for the environment, Pawel's contemplation what the hotel he eventually build would be like, to their fathers' who continued a life of conflict as part of the enchilada.

Then Gloria said, Pawel, do you want to know something?"

"What?"

Vice-principal Ed Ami who is supervising tonight's dance, recently asked me for a date."

Surprised, Pawel objected to such a thing happening. "But he's eleven years older than you are."

"That's the point, "Gloria said and went on, "And he keeps telling me about the Purple Grape winery his parents own in Penticton, British Columbia. He keeps talking about *Pride of the Okanagan* – a 1919 vintage wine that his parents have vinted and how popular it is. He also says, and thinks of this, if one drinks enough of the wine, they will see a ghost."

"Don't be foolish in accepting a date with Mr. Ami," Pawel protested. "I realize, he like yourself, is an environmentalist and both of French ancestry, but if he calls me a Buhunk one more time, I'm going to flatten his face."

Surprised, Gloria said, "You what?"

"Flatten his face."

"I wouldn't do that or else you'll get the strap like Walter Barba did last week."

In that particular incident Walter who sat behind Kwitka in class, cut of a lock of her hair with a pair of scissors. Kwitka turned around and with a ruler smacked Walter across the face.

"I didn't think you would do it a second time," Ami said to Walter in the vice-principal's office.

"Do what?"

"Cut Kwitka's hair," Ami lashed out at Walter calling him everything under the sun.

Asserting himself Walter said, "Shut up you fat pig. I didn't hurt Kwitka."

"Fat pig?" Ami said. "I'll show you who is a fat pig."

Ami took a foot long ruler from his desk and struck Walter's palm ten times on each hand. When Walter jerked his hand back Ami made Walter hold it out again and there were three more, "Smack, smack and smack."

When the smacking was done, and Walter's palms turned red, he said, "You didn't make me cry."

"Go stand in the corner for one-half hour, it may," Ami said.

It was several minutes before midnight when Pawel and Gloria returned to the dance and Vice-principal Ed Ami, a baldheaded, muscular man with a pug nose, holding a Master's degree from the University of British Columbia, was anxiously waiting at the entrance door.

As Pawel and Gloria approached the entrance Ami said to both of them, "I'm concerned."

"About what?" Pawel asked.

"That you have been doing something which is not permitted on school grounds. Let me smell your breath."

And when he did, Ami continued, "Just as I thought.  Chokecherry wine, wasn't it?"

When Pawel admitted that he and Gloria consumed a bottle, Ami gave the couple a stern look and said, "Okay, we'll discuss it first thing Monday morning."


On Monday morning when Ami asked Pawel what else he and Gloria were doing Friday night besides drinking chokecherry wine. Pawel in jest said, "We were playing strip poker."

"Strip poker? The school board will hear about this."

In a flash Pawel corrected himself and said that the *strip poker* comment may have not been the right choice of words, Ami screamed, "Aha, sure, you Buhunks are all the same."

"You called me a Bohunk!" Pawel shot back and followed the comment with a hard punch to Ami's head. Blows were exchanged. Having taken boxing lesions from Josiah Alexander, Pawel came out as the winner despite Ami's burly size.

With blood streaming from his nose Ami screamed at Pawel again, "I don't want you back at this school until you hear from the School Board."

Two days later, the disciplinary committee of the school board met with Pawel and his parents. After reading Ami's report out loud the committee chairman said, "Well, Pawel Kowalchuk, what have you got to say for yourself? Did you punch the vice-principal?"

"I did after Gloria Gateau and I enjoyed a bottle of chokecherry wine on a nearby vacant lot."

"How about you and Gloria playing strip poker?"

"That was a mistake. I shouldn't have said that."

Turning to Evdokia the chairman asked, "Mrs. Kowalchuk, do you know what strip poker means?"

"Evdokia shrugged her shoulders, "It's a card game, I guess."

"At seventeen years of age and drinking wine with your son, may mean more than that."

When the meeting finished the end result was that Pawel was suspended for two weeks so he looked at the chairman and said, "Please give me a break."

No break was given.

"If that is the case, I'll finish my grade twelve through correspondence."

The following day Pawel ordered his lessons.


On the same day that Pawel ordered correspondence lessons Evdokia received another letter from her sister in Ukraine. In part the letter read:

Dear Evdokia,

"Famine has now spread throughout Ukraine, creating horrible conditions. I saw many people near Lvov and those lying in Kiev's Golden State Square being picked up and thrown into trucks like pieces of garbage. There were other people in the park, half alive and bloated, and if I told someone I in turn was told to keep quiet and say I didn't see it. "But I saw family farms being seized as Russian soldiers parched themselves on towers guarding crops. The soldiers didn't want people to steal from the fields, and if they got caught, you would never see them again.

More in my next letter."

Filipa in Lvov (1935)

By now Gloria and Pawel were seeing each other regularly despite disapproval of their parents, especially Pawel's mother. It was also rumored that Abe Goldman and Sister Raphael were contacting each other too, but no one could prove it.

Pawel and Gloria also showed a keen interest in Social Credit under the aegis of the popular and persuasive orator William Aberhart, whom they had met before and heard on the radio. And like Aberhart, Pawel and Gloria felt conditions were ripe for a change in both the provincial and federal governments.

They got politically involved. If their parents' couldn't change the political system they and Aberhart would try.

In the province of Alberta William Aberhart and R. B. Bennett were familiar names. Aberhart had a radio program emanating from CFCN Calgary and Prime Minister Bennett who spoke in Ottawa about a *New Deal* he was going to implement and get the economy moving and people back to work.

In December Aberhart announced: "At the next provincial election reliable, honorable, bribe-proof businessmen who definitely lay off their political affiliation, will be asked to support the Social Credit party in every constituency."

Soon mid-week programs on *Back to the Bible* were featuring short plays written by Aberhart and his student Ernest Manning. The central character of the drama was the *Man from Mars*, a creature who could not understand why people in Alberta had not already instituted Social Credit.

After listening to several of the programs, Pawel said to his parents, "Mom and dad, I'm going to seek the Social Credit candidacy for the Bonnyville riding."

"You what?" the parents said simultaneously.

"I'm going to seek the Social Credit candidacy for the Bonnyville constituency in the upcoming provincial election."

When the parents suggested Pawel had no chance of winning the nomination because he was still a teenager, had been expelled from school and not French-speaking, Pawel quoted Aberhart who often said, "You don't have to know all about Social Credit before you vote for it. All you have to do is push the button and you get the light."

"Well, son," Evdokia went on, "I hope you do see the light because there are at least two other candidates who plan to run against you."

"Pawel, you haven't got a chance because you haven't got a degree or experience," Roman continued.

"Don't worry about my education. Most Ukrainians aren't educated. But tell me who the other prospective candidates are?"

"The first to announce his candidacy is magistrate Alphonse Mussault. He's well known in Bonnyville," Roman replied.

Curious to know, Pawel asked, "And the second?"

"Your vice-principal, Ed Ami."

Pawel almost choked on a piece of holubtsi he was enjoying, "Magistrate Mussault and vice-principal Ami, you say. I agree they are formidable candidates but I'm eighteen years of age now and think I can beat them."

Roman glanced at Pawel with puzzlement. "You are a stubborn young man but I guess you have to start from somewhere and if you lose, you haven't lost much but have gained experience."

Evdokia also relented and wished Pawel the best of luck. Pawel was pleased he had obtained his parent's consent to enter politics.

"And you know something else that Aberhart once said?" Pawel continued.

"What?"

"It's the rooster that makes the noise and the hen lays the eggs."

Evdokia burst out with laughter but it did not last long because Roman reminded Pawel that if he's going to pursue the nomination, he needed a campaign manager.

"I have already taken care of that."

"Really? Who is he?"

"It's not a he. It's Gloria Gateau who will help me as soon as she graduates from High School in June."

Hearing the election date Evdokia said, "To me Gloria is more like tree swallow than an election campaign manger. Tree swallows, in the event you don't know, kill male offspring's of male rivals and even believe in divorce. Furthermore, French girls don't enjoy eating borstch. I thought your dream was to own an inn on a shore of a beautiful lake and not to be a politician."

"Mom, politics will help me in achieving my goal. It's through politics that one gets to meet influential people." Pawel said.

The first time Pawel was involved in an election had been when he ran for the presidency    of the Palm school student council and Gloria defeated him.

By the time nomination day came in May, tensions ran high among each party organizers accusing one anther of one falsehood followed by another.

The candidate for the Farmers of Alberta
Party even had the gumption to say, "What's
wrong with you people in Bonnyville? You
need your brains adjusted if you allow an
uneducated Ukrainian teenager be your Social
Credit candidate?"
Pawel however, felt confident, that with hard
work and visiting each voter personally, he
had an excellent chance to win. His plan was
to criss-cross the Bonnyville riding at least
twice and knock on as many doors as
possible.

On nomination day Pawel was surprised at the
large number of people who showed interest
in politics – they filled the stuffy High School
gymnasium in order to cast their ballot.
Actually the mood among voters was chaotic
with young and old clogging the school
hallways.
"I'm as surprised as you are," Gloria said
while giving Pawel a reassuring squeeze. "I
think we did an excellent job selling
membership cards but you know elections,
voters are fickle and one of the other
candidates may have the nomination stacked."
"I know.

But in the last week I campaigned real hard. Watch we'll have our side come by busloads." Pawel recognized many faces he had spoken too. Among them were his father's friends: Nick and Olga Barba, Josiah Alexander, Mr. and Mrs. Lee Wong and Chief Dion from the Kehewin Indian Reserve. The Chief was present mostly for moral support because at that time Indians didn't have the right to vote.

Pawel felt nervous when he saw the large number of people at the rally. There were men standing in the back against the wall and even chairs had to be placed in the aisles. As soon as the clock struck 8:00 p. m. and the chairman stood up to introduce the candidates, a hush fell on the gymnasium. The chairman explained the rules and told the audience that each candidate was allowed twenty minutes to speak with a rebuttal of five, and that the meeting would end with a question period from the audience and finally, casting of a secret ballot.
The chairman then said that a draw had been made in advance and vice-principal Ed Ami would speak first, Alphonse Mussault, second and Pawel third.

When Ami stood up there was a mild applause. He began his speech in French and then switching to English. Ami outlined his priorities and vision for Alberta, which were, "Get people working."
Ami condemned the United Farmers of Alberta who were in power, stressing more provincial aid for municipalities so they could build roads and bridges. Ami also talked about the environment and said that in not a distant future there would be no lakes suited for public recreation because of pollution.

"For example, in Penticton, B. C. where I come from, Okanagan and Skaha lakes are already polluted with domestic sewage. Soon we won't be able to swim there or use the beaches."
Near the end of his speech Ami switched back to French, highlighting what he had said in English. When Ami finished his speech and sat down there was a mild polite applause but Pawel could see that many remained silent.
Alphonse Mussault spoke next and unlike Ami began his speech in English, which drew a substantial applause.

He was a hard-fisted conservative who knew lots about Scripture and liked to quote them during Citizenship Day.

Mussault began, "I stand before you as the local candidate. As most of you know I'm the local magistrate and a businessman. My family operated an insurance agency in Bonnyville since 1908 when the first Oblate Fathers came here.

I have served the Bonnyville constituency in many ways. Besides being a magistrate I served on the school board, was a government inspector, a municipal councilor and a member of the Knights of Columbus. I do not have the education of Ed Ami but on the other hand I'm no teenager either."

In the audience there was a silent movement and some started coughing knowing that the last remark was directed at Pawel.

Mussault continued, "I do not have wealth and like many of you in the audience, because of the present economy, I'm broke most of the time. I have ten children with one son in a seminary to become a priest. This may surprise you but one of my daughters is a nun and you may know her better as Sister

Raphael, the principal at the Bonnyville High School. She took her vows in Winnipeg." There was mild applause but Pawel could sense it wasn't genuine. He conceded however, that the opponents were articulate and formidable prospects for the Social Credit candidacy.

He listened intently as Mussault then spoke about the Social Credit theory and twenty-five dollars the party promised to get the economy moving.

Mussault also spoke about high interest rates, mortgages, bankruptcies and foreclosures. Near the end of his speech switched to speaking French and highlighted what he had said in English earlier. Mussault ended his speech to a sustained applause.

When the chairman rose to introduce him, Pawel felt nervous and wished he had written a speech. He began by quoting Aberhart, "It's the rooster that makes the noise but the hen lays the eggs. I would like to be your hen for the next five years as a member of the Social Credit Party in the legislature in Edmonton." The comment drew sparks of laughter from the crowd and having overcome his initial nervousness Pawel proceeded, "My parents came from Ukraine and it's a known fact that I got expelled from high school by the first speaker.  My parents have no wealth either but a lot of hope for a prosperous future. That is why I'm asking you to nominate me as your candidate and have Social Credit win the next election on August 22nd.

There was applause but Pawel noticed some didn't join in. He continued, "I do not apologize for being Ukrainian and now eighteen years of age. I do not apologize that my mother wears a *babushka*, my father a sheepskin coat or that some call Ukrainians *Bohunks* or *Scum of Europe*.

*I*f elected I intend to fight for the rights of the farmer, businessman, the unemployed irrespective of their nationality."

There was deafening applause after Pawel spoke briefly in Ukrainian, Polish and French. The applause quieted down just long enough for Pawel to say, "If it's not my destiny to be your Social credit candidate, then I will support and work with the winner.

But whatever you do next August remember to get out your neighbors and friends to vote and defeat the United Farmers of Alberta."

Pawel sat down to continuing applause.
This was followed by a five-minute rebuttal
and a brief question period. After the question
period concluded the chairman ordered
scrutinizers to pass a hat around for a
collection to cover the cost of renting the
gymnasium. When this was done ballots were
distributed to elect the candidate.

It took an hour minutes before the secret
ballots were counted and results announced.
During that time those who had cast their
ballot stood around drinking coffee and
gossiped. As soon as the chairman switched
on the microphone everyone was seated and
there was another hush in the crowd.
"Ladies and gentlemen," the chairman began
and continued, "The Social Credit candidacy
results for the Bonnyville riding are as
follows:"
There was dead silence in the gymnasium.
"In third place, Ed Ami with 99 votes."
There was a sense of dejection on Ami's face
and those of his supporters.
"In second place," the chairman continued,
"Alphonse Mussault with 117 votes."

The crowd burst into sustained applause knowing a second ballot wasn't necessary and this was confirmed when the chairman announced, "Congratulations to Pawel Kowalchuk who had 232 votes."

The announcement had the festive air of a victory party as Mussault immediately stepped up and congratulated Pawel but that wasn't so with Ed Ami who stalked out of the gymnasium.

"I'm happy for you, Pawel. Congratulations." Gloria said as a crowd of well-wishers, including Gloria's parents, gathered around Pawel.

"I'm happy for both of us," Pawel said and followed with giving Gloria a hug and a kiss on her cheek, "I wish you all the luck in the world in your nursing studies at the University of Alberta in Edmonton."

There was little time to talk about Gloria's career, for the moment at least, as Roman, Evdokia and Kwitka did their share of congratulating too. Even on an occasion like this Jacques and Roman did speak to each other but their wives exchange pleasantries and were jubilant that Pawel had won the nomination and Gloria would be his manager.

In making his acceptance speech, which was brief, Pawel began with, "Friends! I want to make it absolutely clear that Mr. Ami and Mr. Masscult's contribution to the community will not be forgotten," and continued, "I'm aware that because of my age and Ukrainian heritage I'll be judged by the French-speaking and Anglo Saxon majority. I want to make it perfectly clear that I will accept all points of view and admit it's a moment of triumph. I'm looking forward toward seeing William Aberhart when he comes to Bonnyville in July.

In the meantime I solicit everyone's view and concerns on how to get rid of poverty that's among us.

I also solicit help in manning the local campaign headquarters. Again thank you for coming out and choosing me as your Social Credit candidate. I'm certain we can give the old line parties a good fight. ``

Next day Pawel picked up a copy of the *Nouvelle* newspaper to see what coverage it gave him.

There were two front-page headlines. The first read: Teenager Nominated Social Credit Candidate.
The second: Vice Principal Ed Ami Named Principal at a High School in Penticton, British Columbia.

# CHAPTER ELEVEN

During the month of June the Gateau family found itself sitting in the auditorium of the Bonnyville High School. Gloria was graduating. She was wearing a blue suit with high-heeled shoes, both her mother ordered through the Eaton's catalogue. Gloria had a look of maturity as Principal Sister Raphael presented her with a diploma and said, "Gloria Gateau, you have reached adulthood. Go and realize your dream."
Although Pawel did not take part in the graduation exercise because he completed his grade twelve through correspondence he showed up in his father's pickup. As soon as the ceremony was over he presented Gloria with a graduation gift, a bracelet, with the word *Gloria 1935* inscribed on it.
The following day Pawel, Gloria and a dozen of their closest friends whooped and screeched as they careened down Main Street of Bonnyville and followed a road to a Moose Lake cabin where an election party was organized, Gloria drew up a schedule for Pawel to follow and picked an office that was

in the front of an empty store, which closed a year earlier.  The rent was low, parking was plentiful and it was a short walk from Main Street to the High School where the ballots would be eventually be counted during the election.

The furniture was cheap, rented, and consisted primarily of folding tables and wooden chairs. The walls were covered with large photos of William Aberhart and Pawel. Another wall had a chart of the constituency breakdown by polling stations and how residents in each voted during the previous election.

On Monday morning Pawel did not hold a garage sale or eat bananas to cure his ills but posed for photographs with farmers, lumberjacks, fishermen and businessmen. In the evening he and Gloria knocked on doors and ate a variety of dishes in the process, ranging from pea soup, goulash, pyrohy to oriental noodles as they campaigned vigorously.

When the campaign began in earnest Pawel's main opponent, Jean Boisvert of the United Farmers of Alberta, accused Pawel of campaigning night and day to which Pawel

replied, "That's what my parents taught me, never to give up and work long hours."
On Sundays Pawel attended mass, civic functions and outdoor picnics. He competed in three-legged, wheelbarrow and egg-spoon carrying races.

While in the outlying villages he made it a point to visit the parish priest but the most important event, which he attended, was the July 1, Dominion Day celebrations in Bonnyville. Here he took part in the morning parade, attended an Indian pow-wow, a horse race and a baseball tournament that featured teams from Bonnyville, St. Paul, Glendon, Ardmore, Cold Lake and a team of Indians from the Kehewin Reserve.

Throughout all these events Pawel shook as many hands as he could but the event that came as soon as the sun set, a dance at the community hall, he enjoyed the most spinning around the floor with Gloria to the polka, kulomyeka and two-step.
Aberhart's political rally in Bonnyville began with everyone singing *Oh God Our Help in Ages Past* in the High School auditorium.

Next Pawel introduced the preacher to the audience who began speaking immediately by catching the attention of the crowd and holding it spellbound for the next hour and one-half with quotes from the *Scripture* and catch phrases like, "It's the rooster that makes the noise but the hen lays the eggs," Big shots are to blame for poverty in Alberta." and "Social Credit is like electricity. You don't have to know it to use it."

In simple language Aberhart described to his audience how to feed, clothe and shelter, at least with the bare necessities of life. After briefly speaking about the significant parts of his religious-economic doctrine, Aberhart launched his appeal for action to end Alberta's state of poverty in the age of plenty.

As Aberhart spoke poverty-bitten families burst into tears and women swooned as his eloquence soared to a climax amid shouts, "We want William Aberhart! We want Pawel Kowalchuk! Let's pray for them!"

Aberhart then lashed out at the old-line parties with sarcasm for their ineptitude in the face of a Depression.

At the end, Pawel thanked Aberhart for coming to Bonnyville as many rushed up stage saying they would vote for Social Credit because Aberhart was a, *Savior.*"

Journalists covering the rally found a different impression of Aberhart. One reporter wrote, "Even sitting down Aberhart is an impressive figure and once he rose to speak the audience was his until he chose to stop talking."
A second wrote, "Aberhart told people what they wanted to hear, that heaven and earth were to be had for the making. Aberhart preached that under Social Credit there would be better distribution of wealth without disturbing private ownership and that he was definitely an anti-Communist."
A third journalist compared Aberhart to the prophet Elijah who received his revelation from heaven. "Aberhart has a loud voice, a noble brow and a massive frame. He is a practical pedagogue and a preacher."
All journalists doubted however, what Aberhart had said or that everything would be wonderful if he was right.
The journalists called Aberhart's Social Credit formula *Funny Money* and doubted that

Social Credit would work and Social Credit had no chance of winning the election.

As journalists followed Aberhart across the province electioneering, most newspapers became convinced Aberhart was more hopeless than any leader they heard and that Pawel was just as hopeless in winning an election as his leader

But on August 22, 1935 Social Credit won a majority with 56 of the 63 seats and Pawel was one of them, winning the riding of Bonnyville where at a gathering of faithful he said, "The way people have shown confidence in me is truly humbling. Right now I have two goals: to represent this riding the best I can and to eliminate poverty."

The day after the election a number of people lined up outside Social Credit headquarters in Calgary to collect their $25 dividends but they weren't available.

When the *Nouvelle* reporter asked why he voted Social Credit Roman replied, "When I first met Aberhart he got me out of jail in 1928. I immediately realized he was a good man."

When the same reporter asked Nick Barba the same question his reply was, "When I heard Aberhart urge everyone to pull together an amazing change took place in my life. At the political rally I cried out, 'Let's pray for William Aberhart and Pawel Kowalchuk' And as everyone prayed I knew the country was going to be saved."

Lee Wong told the same reporter, "If we are to fulfill Confucius's vision for man we must take up Social Credit and I may even get to operate my restaurant again."

Mr. Wong was convinced Confucius inspired Aberhart but if he didn't know much about Social Credit and that was all right, because premier-elect Aberhart would take care of everything.

When the same reporter interviewed Evdokia she said, "I know Aberhart is a good man and will teach our son everything there is to know about politics. Now if we can get rid of Prime Minister R. B. Bennett and the Conservative government in Ottawa during the October election, things are bound to get better."

While Canadians were waiting for the federal election Pawel familiarized himself with Social Credit policy but found there were no $25 dividends to distribute. He rented a one-bedroom apartment in Edmonton that overlooked the parliament buildings and the North Saskatchewan River. It was the same time that Gloria was admitted to the University of Alberta Nursing School in Edmonton and live in the women's dormitory. While Pawel attended to legislative matters Gloria attended nursing classes. They communicated with each other frequently and on weekends Gloria slipped into his apartment to have a nap. She would enter the bedroom and slide between the sheets of the canopy bed. Within minutes Pawel crawled under the sheets too and both fell into a dreamless sleep.

As soon as Aberhart won the election, he ran in a by-election in the Okotoks-High Prairie riding, and after winning it, became the premier of Alberta.
It didn't take Pawel long to realize that being a member of the legislature wasn't a full time job but the pay was substantial thus enabling,

without over extending himself, to buy a new 1935 two-door blue Ford car.

Pawel also made substantial down payments not only on the car but also on a Massy Harris tractor, a hay mower and a John Deere binder for his parents. The tractor was used to break more land during the month of May. Haying time took place during June and July.

The meadow on the Kowalchuk's farm lay next to a slough facing south. As there was some rain that spring the grass was golden green in color and increased in size as it grew closer to the water where ducks, mud hens, killdeers and red-wing blackbirds nested, muskrats found shelter, cattail grew tall and frogs floated on lily pads.

With the mower, pulled by a team of horses, Roman sat on the seat of the machine and cut the grass leaving it to dry. Once the grass was dry it was raked with a hay rake, left in windrows and then into piles. The next step was to deliver the hay and stack it near the barn. The alternative was to compact the hay into a *slide* that resembled large loaf of bread and pulled by a team of four horses.

Roman pitched the hay and Evdokia tramp each forkful until the hay got higher and higher.

Most of the time Evdokia worked in silence but on occasions she would stop and take a rest, wipe sweat from her face and say, "There must be a better way of making a living than farming."
Once the slide was completed work would begin on another. Up to fifteen slides of hay side by side was a common sight near sloughs in east central Alberta.

When it came to harvesting, the binder was delivered by an implement dealer and in late August pulled by a team of four horses. Roman sat on a seat overlooking the machine at times whipping a horse that was slower than the other three. While Roman was operating the binder and guiding the horses, Evdokia and Kwitka did the stooking. As soon as the stocks of grain were dry and threshing began, things went a little easier for Kwitka as she helped her mother with the baking and cooking.

When Angus Marx, a neighbor who owned the threshing machine but not the tractor to run it, because the transmission conked out, Roman's Massy Harris was used to energize the machine to thresh the wheat, barley and oats at the Kowalchuk homestead. Roman and several neighbors hauled the bundles in a hayrack to the threshing machine placed near a granary and if one had a substantial acreage there would be at least two and even more. Like Roman and the threshing crew, Evdokia and Kwitka rose early in the morning to milk the cows, feed the hogs and help prepare breakfast. At 8:00 a. m. when the threshing crew, which often slept in the hayloft, went into the field, with Kwitka's help, Evdokia washed the dishes, made apple and pumpkin pies, prepared the vegetables and put a roast in the oven.

At noon, the threshing crew had dinner and the horses that hauled the sheaves to the threshing machine were fed. Roman checked the grain in the granary and Evdokia was on the run again preparing supper.

After supper, Evdokia and Kwitka milked the cows, separated the cream from the milk and got ready for breakfast again. With luck, if the weather stayed dry and sunny, and the threshing machine didn't break down, the threshing would be finished in several days and the same crew would move to the next neighbor until all harvesting in the area was done. And when it was, the farmers sold the grain to an elevator agent and then pay off their debts that they incurred during the summer.

Even before threshing of the grain began, Prime Minister Bennett made a series of speeches to the nation announcing the most radical program of economic reforms, including: unemployment insurance, social security, a minimum wage law and provisions for a shorter work week.

On October 24, 1935 however, Roman and Evdokia turned on the radio and were delighted when the announcer read a news bulletin that said, "Mackenzie King today defeated R. B. Bennett at the polls. Voters showed little interest in the Conservative Party New Deal. Final count is as follows:

Liberals 171, Conservatives 79, Social Credit 17, CCF 7 and the Reconstruction Party, 1."

# CHAPTER TWELVE

After the defeat of Bennett's Conservative government was announced, the radio announcer read a news bulletin several days later, which was more tragic in the years ahead. The announcer intoned that Germany, under Adolph Hitler, had denounced provisions of the League of Nations established after World War 1, and was building a naval fleet and increasing the size of its army. While Hitler's popularity in Germany was increasing, the Berlin Olympics were held in 1936 where Jesse Owens won a record three gold medals but Hitler refused the Black athletes hand.

It was the same time that another Negro, Joe Louis, became heavyweight boxing champion of the world, which made Josiah Alexander to comment, " Now, if Black people were only allowed to play professional baseball."

Pawel showed a keen interest in government affairs and was developing a quick and an imaginative mind, a capacious memory and an intense capacity for hard work.

Yet with all these plus qualities Pawel's character contained certain flaws that made him unfitted for power and statesmanship. To his closest friends he was charming and vivacious; he could also be temperamental and vindictive.

But the quality that made Pawel least to be a politician was that he wanted to build an inn by a lake and frequently was provoked into impulsive acts. On several occasions he openly admitted, "I'd rather own an inn than be a member of the legislature."

Pawel's comments were made on the same day that Evdokia completed her chores, walked into the house and said to Roman, "Where is Kwitka?"

"I don't know. She's probably out with Walter Barba."

"I just talked to his mother and she says Walter is at home studying."

By now Kwitka had become a brazen young woman with a nasal voice, constantly singing pop tunes of the day to anyone who would listen. She was developing a voluptuous body and the way she accented her femininity drew the ire of her parents but not young men.

After playing the piano for several minutes Evdokia went to the cupboard and pulled out a piece of cheese that she made the day before. She looked towards Roman and said, "Do you want a piece?"

Roman nodded gratefully.

She cut a piece with a butcher knife and sat at the kitchen table with a worried expression. Her eyes grew as large as hen's eggs. While glancing at a clock on the windowsill she said, "It will be dark soon. Kwitka should be been home an hour ago."

"Don't worry," Roman said. "Kwitka will be home any minute now."

Evdokia felt tears coming down her cheeks. She moved her chair next to Roman's and placed her hands on his, "There are times I imagine something terrible will happen to our daughter."

"Sometimes I get those feelings too. There's no doubt Kwitka is an attractive young woman," Roman replied.

As soon as Roman said those words, there was a knock on the door and a policeman informed the worrying parents that Kvitka had been found in the park sexually assaulted.

"Two teenage boys have been arrested and charged. A trial will have to be held," the officer said.

This wasn't the first time Kwitka had experienced a trauma. Another time occurred when this bright and intelligent young woman was going through a change in attitude. But she had parents who were strict and thought her hair and apparel makeup was the least spectacular a teenager could express individuality.

Roman and Evdokia had no second thoughts about going for a weekend to visit Pawel in Edmonton and leaving Kwitka home alone. Besides there were neighbors who would tattle if something should go amiss. Then three days before the planned trip, Evdokia was summoned to the Bonnyville High School where the principal, Sister Raphael, asked if the parents knew about a party planned at the Kowalchuk residence.

"A party at our farm?" Evdokia exploded. "Who's putting on the party?"

"Yes, while you and your husband is away Kwitka is putting one on," Sister Raphael said and then showed Evdokia a poster she had found on the school bulletin board, earlier."

"You tell Kwitka that there will be no party at our residence," Evdokia said and after she returned home, she and Roman were on the verge of thinking that it might be okay to visit Pawel. Then the following day, a friend of Kwitka's turned up with a poster and asked Evdokia, "Isn't this where the Kowalchuk's live?"

It was, and Evdokia became angry.

Apparently Kwitka and her friends had gone beyond the school bulletin board advertising the bash. There were also posters on Main Street in Bonnyville. At that time Evdokia made Kwitka and her friends spend a long afternoon pulling down posters and Sister Raphael agreed to announce that anyone showing up at the Kowalchuk's residence would be met by the parents holding a baseball bat.

The tactic worked, but after the poster escapade, Roman and Evdokia agreed there should be some kind of punishment for Kwitka but not in a physical sense such as a willow stick across her rear-end or long-time grounding.

It was decided that Kwitka should be placed at the Assumption Convent while attending High School.
Kwitka raised no objection.

At the convent Kwitka was initially frightened. The nuns, especially the Superior, Sister Therese, were stern and forbidding in their religious habits.
But they taught catechism and bit-by-bit through therapy, Kwitka was losing her fear of being raped again and waiting for a trial to take place. Kwitka liked being clean, not like some of the girls who stayed at the convent while attending High School and bathing only once a week.The convent actually was a nice place where only women lived.
"Without stupid boys," Kwitka described the place, "My classmates are kind and generous."
The girls staying at the convent did charity work in their spare time: run errands, collect clothing for the poor and visit patients at the hospital. But they needed more spice in their life so one day when the nuns washed their clothes and hung them outside Kwitka

decided to hide the under garments inside the church.

The nuns searched for their garments all day and believing someone outside the convent did the hiding felt the culprit would end up in hell.

The following Sunday, the Kowalchuk's attended the early morning mass and Kwitka became so nervous that she couldn't sing or pray. She almost fainted when Father Lapointe opened the box that kept the communion wafers and found the nuns' underpants and braziers inside.

Despite the misdemeanor, Sister Raphael always liked Kwitka because she was jovial, had a sense of humor and received high marks. Besides, Father Lapointe had written her a letter commending Kwitka for her devout attendance and service to the church, not like many other young women who spent more time in front of a mirror than on their knees.

Father Lapointe expressed the hope that Sister Raphael would find a way to reward the poor Ukrainian girl for devotion by offering a scholarship to Alberta Normal School in Edmonton where teachers' were taught.

The scholarship was given each year to one student whose record for scholastic and religious achievement was deemed the most worthy by a committee. This year it was Kwitka's turn if she decided to become a teacher and this morning she would have to give Sister Raphael her answer.

After Kwitka said that she would accept the scholarship Sister Raphael said, "Its God's mercy you will be dispensing. So you have decided to become a teacher, have you?"

"Yes, sister."

"Why?"

Kwitka shrugged her shoulders. "I don't know, I guess I never really thought about it."

"Was it always your ambition to be a teacher, even when you were a little child?"

Kwitka shook her head.

"Being a teacher is hard work. You'll have little time for yourself. And when you attend Normal School you'll have to study day and night. Your boyfriend may not like that."

"But I have no boyfriend." Kwitka said.

"But you came to school parties with Walter Barba. Isn't he your boyfriend?"

"No sister, Walter isn't my boyfriend, it's only his mother's wish that he was."

"I understand, "Sister Raphael said. "I once had a boyfriend and my parents were against us going out together. In my case however, it was different."

"How was it different?"

"I'm Catholic and my boyfriend at the time was Jewish. Is there anything you would rather be than a teacher? Perhaps a nun like myself?"

Kwitka wasn't prepared to take vows of chastity and poverty however, and when it came to obedience she already had run-ins with her parents and nuns themselves.

"No, I would like to entertain people."

Sister Raphael smiled. "And knowing you as I do, you would be good at it."

Kwitka spent weekends on the farm instead of the convent. When Sunday came, because of the sexual assault, she was reluctant to attend mass.

"Because people stare at you? Is that the reason?" Roman asked.

Kwitka nodded her head.

"Would you go if I came with you?"

Kwitka looked into her father's eyes and saw true love there.

"Yes, Daddy."

"All right. Get dressed while I start the pickup."


There was a buzz of surprise as Roman and Kwitka genuflected while entering the church and walked down the aisle towards a pew. The choir was already singing *Gloria in Excelsis Deo* while Father Lapointe stood at the lectern to begin the mass.

On one of the stained windows the Holy Ghost looked down on the Virgin Mary, another window showed her kneeling before the Infant Jesus, and behind the tabernacle there was a wood carving of St. Louis, one eminent for piety and virtue and the patron saint of the town of Bonnyville.

For his homily Father Lapointe gave a brief outline of social history: the Garden of Eden, the Tower of Babel, cities burning, people dying and respect for the Almighty.

Kwitka listened intently as the priest said that God loved children, healed the blind and had chosen people to be poor.

Kwitka, although religious found it difficult however, to imagine what the Holy Ghost looked like and why God had chosen her parents to be poor or her to be raped. Through the corner of his eye Roman could see heads twisting and turning as the mass progressed. But as bad as it had been inside the church it was worse when the mass ended and Kwitka and her father came outside. The curious had time to gather on the front steps and see a massive bruise on Kwitka's face.

"It's over now," Roman said as he and Kwitka left the church and walked towards where the pickup was parked and two young men hung around and thought it was sport to urinate on the tires, crush cigarettes on the fenders and paint graffiti on the pickup's flat surface. The boys fell silent as the Kowalchuk's approached the pickup and nearby the boys were staring and making snide remarks about foreigners entering Canada.

Roman stared back at them and their eyes fell before his. Pointing towards the pickup one boy who identified himself as Rene Lambert, snickered, another, whose name was, Marcel Mercier, giggled. Abruptly, Roman let go Kwitka's arm and came closer to the boys who looked at him in surprise, the snickering, giggling had died down.

Shaking his fist at Rene and Marcel, Roman asked, "What are the joke boys? Tell me so that I can laugh with you."

The boys stared at Roman and then looked down at their feet.

"Get off this street," Roman said and went on, "If I ever catch you urinating on my pickup again or making snide remarks about me or any member of my family, I'll tear you up with my bare hands."

Rene, the taller of the two youths, whose eyes were sly and insolent, took a step towards Roman and said, "Canada is a free country and we can stay here if we like.

The resentment in Roman suddenly exploded. He seized Rene by the jacket and forced him to his knees. "Free for you to stand here and choose who you'll assailt next."

Rene cringed, the insolence gone from his face, and then said; "You will have to prove it in court that we screwed Kwitka."
They could say that about his teenage daughter and there was nothing he could do that could change the fact. Slowly Roman released his grip on Rene's jacket and flung him away from him. Roman surveyed the boys, looking from one to the other. "They are only boys," he told himself.
He once was a boy and the one's he had just reprimanded perhaps weren't the guilty ones. If anyone was guilty it was himself because he should have listened to Evdokia and placed Kwitka in a convent the year before.

After Roman and Kwitka arrived home, they changed clothing and sat on the steps outside the house enjoying a light breeze when Kwitka said, "Well, Dad, how is it going?"
"I don't understand it. Homesteading is the pits and there are no jobs available."
"Maybe it will soon improve?" Kwitka said.
"I hope so. I thought with the election of Mackenzie King as prime minister, things would improve but his promises weren't kept."

Roman made himself more comfortable and continued, "By the way Kwitka, I didn't tell your mother this but I went to see Father Lapointe yesterday."

"To discuss that I hid Mother Superior's panties and a brazier inside the church?"

"We discussed that too."

"And what else?"

"The upcoming trial and that the Father won't come to court to testify to your character."

"Why not?"

"Because it's against the rules of the Church and that the boys' parents are pillars in the parish."

How about sisters Raphael and Theresa?"

"They too will not come to court to testify on your behalf."

"How come?" Kwitka said as an ailing feeling came inside her. The lawyer may have been right about the rape incident. Noel Comeau had come to see Roman and Evdokia during the week. At that time Comeau sat down at the kitchen table and said to the two concerned parents, "Mr. Lambert and Mr. Mercier have asked me to see you and say how much they regret what their sons' did to your daughter.

They would like to apologize and make amends for their sons' action, if they can." Roman's face flushed with anger. "In the first place Mr. Comeau that incident you refer to was not an incident. Those two boys sexually assaulted our daughter.

"We know what they did but surely, what purpose would their trial serve accept to call even greater attention to your daughter and remind her of what already must be a painful experience. And what if the boys should be found not guilty?"

Evdokia laughed, "Not guilty? The Lambert and Mercier boys were bragging throughout the entire country that they did it."

"What they said is unimportant. It's what they will say in court that counts. And they may say that Roman assaulted one of the boys in front of the church and also that your daughter led them on by inviting them to a party at your home."

"They will have to prove it in court," Roman said.

"It will be harder for you to disprove that. There are two of them and the only word of your daughter. And they will have as many character witnesses, if not more, as you will have for Kwitka."

In response Evdokia said," It's beginning to sound as if our daughter is on trial, not the boys,"

"Exactly, that's why it is in these cases; the accuser stands to lose more than the accused.

"Our daughter's reputation speaks for itself. I'm certain Father Lapointe and the sisters at the convent and high school will tell you of our Kwitka," Evdokia continued.

The lawyer smiled. ``I doubt it Mrs. Kowalchuk, I doubt it very much. I am authorized by my clients however, to offer Kwitka five-hundred dollars, cash, if you will drop the charges against the boys."

"Five-hundred dollars is a joke. Kwitka's self-respect is worth more than that."

"How about one-thousand? Let's do it this way," Roman said trying to willfully suppress his racing heart.

"How much is it worth to your clients knowing that they may have assaulted another female before Kwitka. Let's settle for two-thousand, and have our little secret buried?"

"You are asking me to divulge confidential client information, an egregious act for a lawyer to make. It would get me disbarred in an instant."

"Well, then you might as well leave, Mr. Comeau," Roman said getting to his feet.

"One cannot buy what already is stolen," The lawyer rose also, took a calling card from his pocket, placed on the table and while walking towards the door said, "You can reach me at my office any time before the trial begins if you should change your mind."

"What do we do now, Daddy?" Kwitka asked back to the present.

Roman shrugged his shoulders. "Father Lapointe also said that he was pleased that you have accepted the scholarship to the Normal School in Edmonton."

Kwitka began to laugh. They refused to give her a good name, yet were willing to give her charity. Kwitka couldn't reconcile the two attitudes. Was one merely to compensate for the other?

Roman looked at anxiously his daughter, "What are you laughing at, Kwitka?"

"I think you should give the lawyer a call."

"Then you'll take the one-thousand dollars?"

Kwitka nodded her head, "And the scholarship to Normal School.

That way you and Mom can buy food for the able while I'm away."

"I won't accept your money."

"You should, Daddy."

Following more coaxing Roman did accept the money. There would be no trial. Roman felt tears rush from his eyes and suddenly pulled his daughter to his side. "Do you love me, Kwitka, even if I have failed you?"

"But you haven't failed me, father." she said while placing her head against his chest.

And they clung to each other, crying there on the steps. Crying but not throwing in the towel like Evdokia's sister, Filipa did in a letter she wrote:

Dear Evdokia,

Since my last letter, millions of Ukrainians have starved to death in Ukraine at the whim of Josef Stalin and millions more exiled to Siberia to work in the forests and mines. This is a war between peasants armed with pitchforks and the Red Army and Secret Police that is carried out mercilessly with no pity for the aged or the young nor for women and children. I've been approached by the Secret Police about my articles.

They say everything I write about the famine and Ukrainians dying is false. In the event you don't receive another letter from me, you can write to my son Bogdan who lives in Kiev.
Filipa in Lvov (1936)

# CHAPTER THIRTEEN

On New Year's Eve 1936/37 the famine
continued in Ukraine while Canadians
gathered at house parties across the country
singing around a piano. The Kowalchuk's,
after doing their chores and having supper;
listened to Evdokia play the piano and Kwitka
sing several tunes.

Near midnight, the family sat around the table
playing cards, and at the same time listen to
the radio waiting for the American broadcast
of the arrival of the New Year in Time Square
in New York City. In many Canadian and
American homes, rugs were rolled back and
couples danced to the music of Guy
Lombardo and the Royal Canadians.

Some were doing the Charleston, although
this craze had passed its peak, while others
were doing the fox trot. The Kowalchuk's had
no room to dance in their home but didn't get
to sleep until 2:00 in the morning.

1937 was a year of dust, thistle, worms, and
more grasshoppers than ever before, and less
rain.

There wasn't any hay, as the meadows and some sloughs had dried up, and little coarse grain to feed the livestock. Many farmers like the Antoniuk's, Goulet's and Wick's finally gave up their homesteads and walked away. Roman and Evdokia stayed, however, but asked for *relief* from the Bonnyville municipality. They like other ethnic immigrants were often rebuffed when the French-speaking secretary said that if they asked for relief, they would be deported. Despite difficult conditions no one wanted to be deported and those that did receive, paid their dues by slashing brush and burning it along municipal roads.

In 1937, much of Pawel's time was taken up with visiting constituents. One afternoon while in Bonnyville he stopped at the Gateau and his parent's residence and announced that he and Gloria were engaged to be married. While at his parent's home he enjoyed a cup of tea with his parents and at the same time turned on the radio when the announcer said, "We interrupt this program to bring you a news bulletin."

Evdokia turned up the volume as the announcer proceeded, "Buckingham Palace has just announced that King Edward V11, the Duke of Windsor and son of King George V, has abdicated the thrown of the British Empire because he loved an American divorcee more. The new king is George V1, the Duke of Windsor's brother. God save the new king."

"But why?" Roman asked.

"Because he loved a divorced American woman more that he loved to be the king of the British Empire."

Then, over a second cup of tea Pawel without warning shocked his parents more than King Edward did by abdicating when he nonchalantly said, "Mom and Dad, I'm going to marry Gloria Gateau."

Surprised, Evdokia said, "You what?"

"Gloria and I are engaged to be married as soon as she graduates in nursing."

Roman took the marriage announcement more casually and said, "Ah ha, this means that Jacques Gateau will come on bended knees and try to make peace with your father and me?"

Jacques Gateau didn't want to seem eager but he was. He grabbed his wife Paulette, by the arm and the couple hurried across the road to congratulate Roman and Evdokia. As soon as they reached the Kowalchuk residence and Roman opened the door Jacques gave Evdokia big hug and to Roman said, "Congratulations, we'll be relatives soon." Roman said, "So?"

"So since your son is marrying our daughter, please allow me to say, let's be friends from this day forward."

Fearing Jacques may be deceiving him and with some pride left, Roman said, "So you think things are about to change since Pawel and Gloria will get married."

"They certainly will, I'll guarantee you."

"No more racial slurs?"

"No more," Jacques replied and grabbed Roman's arm, almost knocking him to the floor and said, "I apologize for my behavior in the past. Please pardon and accept my apology."

Ronan said: "Yes we can, Yes we will."

Evdokia eventually did accept the apology and while discussing the wedding arrangements each enjoyed glasses of chokecherry wine that Roman brought from the cellar.

The reconciliation with Jacques would change Roman's way of life but as soon as the Gateau's left, Evdokia turned to Pawel and made matters worse when she said, "Son, this may offend you but why don't you marry a Ukrainian woman instead? There are many Ukrainians living in Edmonton."

Pawel did not respond. It was quite an ordeal as Evdokia fielded one question, a second and then a third ending with, "Mark my word. If you marry Gloria Gateau, you will never get to build your inn."

"Why not?" Pawel asked.

"Because French women don't like to eat borscht."

Pawel was going to say, 'Thank God for that" but instead used good judgment and said, "Mom, I'm an adult now and who I marry is strictly my business."

Roman agreed. "If Pawel can decide what political party to join he surely should be able to decide who he wants to marry."

He turned to Evdokia, "Why are you surprised that Pawel popped the question?"

"Because marriages between two different cultures seldom work, that's why."

Roman then asked Pawel, "Do you love Gloria?"

"Of course I love her and always will."

"That's all that matters."

When Kwitka found out about the prospect of having a wedding in the family, although she herself said she would never marry, asked Pawel, "Is it going to be French or Ukrainian wedding?"

His reply was, "Both."

"And can I sing at your wedding?"

"Gloria and I would be delighted if you were the soloist."

Roman broke in, "Should I make more chokecherry wine for the occasion?"

"Nah, we'll use the real stuff," Pawel replied and said that while on a tour of parliament buildings he had met several tourists from Penticton, British Columbia and each had said that the city of 25,000 populations situated on the southern edge of Okanagan Lake was an ideal place for a honeymoon."

It was an unusually mild August in 1937 and wild roses were in bloom everywhere but Evdokia had failed to make contact with her sister Filipa in Lvov. Even worse she was also unable to locate her nephew, Bogdan, in the city of Kiev.

It was also the month when Gloria Gateau and Pawel Kowalchuk exchanged vows in the little white colored St. Louis Roman Catholic Church in Bonnyville.

The wedding took place after Gloria graduated as an operating nurse and began her career at the University of Alberta Hospital in Edmonton.

The hospital was near the parliament building and both overlooked a valley and the North Saskatchewan River.

The wedding ceremony began with Father Lapointe reciting the opening prayer in Latin. The first reading was from the Letter of St. Paul to the Corinthians. When it came to the reading of the Gospel everyone stood up and Father Lapointe read from the *Bible* according to St. Mark that dealt with from the beginning of Creation God made male and female.

"For this cause a man shall leave his father and mother and cleave to his wife and the two shall become flesh. Whatever God joined together let no man put asunder. This is the Gospel of the Lord."

The marriage ceremony continued with Father Lapointe saying during the homily, "Dear friends.

You have come to this church so that the Lord may seal and strengthen Pawel and Gloria's love in the presence of the Church's minister and the community.

Please Jesus; abundantly bless this love which in our community is unusual in that it involves two people of different cultures – French and Ukrainian."

This time Father Lapointe looked directly and Gloria and Pawel. "He has already consecrated you in baptism and now He enriches and strengthens you to assume a special sacrament so that you may assume duties of marriage in mutual and lasting fidelity.

And in the presence of the Church I ask you to state you intentions.

Pawel Kowalchuk and Gloria Gateau, have you come here freely without reservations to give yourselves to each other in marriage?"
Pawel and Gloria appeared nervous, faced each other and Pawel said, "I will."
And then Gloria said, "I will."
Father Lapointe proceeded, "Will you love and honor each other as man and wife for the rest of your days?"
Simultaneously Pawel and Gloria answered, "I will."
"Will you accept children from God, and bring them up according to the law of Christ and the Church?"
Again Pawel and Gloria each said, "I will."
"Since it's your intention to enter into marriage, join your right hands together and declare your consent before God and the Church."
At this point Pawel said, "I, Pawel Kowalchuk take Gloria Gateau to be my wife, to laugh with you in joy, to cry with you in sorrow, to grow with you in love. I will love and honor you all the days of my life."
When it was Gloria's turn she repeated what Pawel had just said.

When she finished Father Lapointe proceeded, "You Pawel Kowalchuk and Gloria Gateau, have declared your consent before the Church. May the Lord in His goodness strengthen your consent and fill both of you with His blessings. What God has joined, men and women must not divide." During communion Kwitka sang *Panis Angelicus* and when the mass ended Pawel kissed Gloria and together they went to the sacristy to sign the register. During their absence Kwitka sang *Ave Maria*.

When it was time for the recessional everyone stood up and then when the newlywed began walking to the front door, there was a sudden rush to clear the church out and spray the bride and groom with confetti and rice. When this was done, everyone as a convoy headed for the Gateau homestead where the reception took place.

Rather than in a car Pawel and Gloria drove off in a horse-drawn carriage. They were sitting at the back on bales of hay, when something startled the horses, causing them to leap forward suddenly Gloria lost her balance and fell backwards, her feet flying into the air and then landing on the ground.

Those watching gasped.

A bystander said, "I hope her injury isn't serious."

But like a knight in shining armour, Pawel came to Gloria's rescue. He scooped her up in his arms and then gave her a hug and a kiss. Those present applauded and cheered until the driver got the horses back in order.

Pawel and Gloria climbed back into the carriage and joined other horse-drawn vehicles, cars, pickups and motorbikes to the Gateau residence where in the kitchen, cream cans of moonshine were hidden and lookouts stood outside in the event of a surprise visit by the Royal Canadian Mounted Police.

It was a relatively large wedding with over one hundred fifty guests present including Paul and Erin White; and Peter and Margaret Black from Winnipeg. During the reception guests congratulated Gloria and Pawel and wished the couple happiness. One of the first to congratulate the bride and groom was the reporter/photographer from the *Nouvelle* newspaper and covered the event for the

Canadian Press news gathering agency. Andre Nadeau had watched Pawel grow into adulthood since he wrote an article about his *Gopher Hole Boutique.*

Nadeau shot photographs of French speaking guests sitting at a table at one end of the house and Ukrainian at another.

Fortunately it turned out to be an extremely pleasant day with plenty of sunshine so Nadeau had a photograph field day later, as guests mingled outside where a platform was built for dancing. A five-piece band played all sorts of Ukrainian and French tunes.

As the celebration continued, the Scotsman, Angus MacDonald who owned the threshing machine, appeared on the dance floor wearing a kilt and on a bagpipe played several Scottish tunes. As soon as MacDonald was through, Josiah Alexander and his wife jumped onto the platform and gave a demonstration of tap-dancing.

Chief Dion and his wife Elizabeth, who performed the *Wedding Dance*, followed them, and when they were through, Lee Wong and his family performed a *Dragon Dance*. But the loudest applause came when Kwitka did a song and dance routine.

While Kwitka was performing, Nadeau shot a photograph of Roman and Jacques sitting at a table over a glass of homebrew chatting, laughing and exchanging anecdotes about farming, grain quotas, livestock prices, politics and that the Depression and the poverty which  continued.
By evening everyone took time out from dancing and singing and served themselves to a buffet-style supper that featured both Ukrainian and French cuisine. They chewed, swallowed, drank, laughed, waved and winked until the presents of all descriptions were put aside to be opened later at home.

The marriage of Gloria and Pawel seemed to be made in heaven but would have to be lived on earth. This, at times would be difficult for the couple that adhered to two different cultures.

Immediately after everyone enjoyed their meal the bride and groom changed into casual clothing, and while the guests kept on dancing, they climbed into Pawel's car, and were on their honeymoon heading for British Columbia. And that was all right because an hour later the RCMP did a surprise search for illegal liquor but didn't find any.

The search failed because those watching outside gave an advance warning. Another tactic used was to have muscular ladies, French and Ukrainian, greet the RCMP constables at the door.

These ladies then hauled the constables onto the dance floor, which gave the kitchen workers a chance to dispose of the moonshine.

"How can I refuse to dance with a lady, especially if she holds me in a powerful grip," said one of the two constables.

As soon as Pawel and Gloria reached Penticton they registered at the Lakeshore Motel, which faced Okanagan Lake, and went to sleep. The following morning, the bride and groom had breakfast put on their bathing suits and relaxed sunbathing at a secluded spot near Okanagan Lake Beach.

It was here that Pawel picked up a piece of driftwood and with it, printed in the crystal sand the words, *This Is Where I Will Build My Inn*.

Pawel then made an acceptable offer for the property and continued enjoying the honeymoon.

When Pawel and Gloria returned to Edmonton two weeks later, friends wanted to know what the trip to British Columbia was like. Gloria's response was, "The scenery is beautiful and Penticton is a wonderful city, but driving on the narrow dirt Big Bend Highway which dangerously follows the Columbia River below, made me nervous. To tell you the truth that part of the honeymoon was frightening."

Meanwhile Premier Aberhart who helped to find the Social Credit Party was unable gain control of Alberta banks by his government but he gained a foothold in the provinces financial industry by creating Alberta Treasury branches in 1938. ATB opened its first branch in the town of Rocky Mountain House and became Aberhart's legacy operating since 2004 as an orthodox financial institution and a crown corporation.

A year following Pawel and Gloria's marriage and the opening of Alberta Treasury Branches the entire world was frightened when Adolph Hitler signed a peace alliance with Russia and then marched on Austria after the collapse of its government. On September 9, 1939, Hitler attacked Poland and World War 2 began. Roman because of an early severe frost-damage was having difficulty harvesting the day Canada entered the war, September 10th. Next day, Roman announced that operating the farm was difficult and spread the word that his 320 acres were for sale and that he and Evdokia wished to move to Penticton, British Columbia which Pawel described as, *God's Country*.

# CHAPTER FOURTEEN

By 1940, Evdokia still had not heard from Bogdan and World War 11 continued as Hitler attacked other parts of Europe including the Ukraine part of the Soviet Union. Hitler's conquests, unequalled since the days of Napoleon, progressed unchallenged so three young men from Bonnyville, Marcel Gateau, Walter Barba and Pawel Kowalchuk left their passionate dreams and ambitions behind by enlisting into the Canadian Armed Forces the same day.

A man of deep religious belief Roman opposed war of any kind all his life.

"We oppose the war too but at the same time we accept the fact that Hitler's ambitions in Europe must be resisted by force," Pawel said.

In an emotionally charged scene, before the three men left by train, each group of parents wished their sons' luck. As the train was about to disappear bound for Edmonton, they cried and prayed for their sons 'safe return.

During Pawel's absence Gloria gave birth to a set of twins. On November 15th Father Lapointe baptized each with the name Joseph and Maurice but the two sons were soon called Joe and Moe most of the time. Before Pawel joined the forces he did not seek reelection for a second term. But because of his involvement earlier had an opportunity to meet influential people. He had already met King George V1 and Queen Elizabeth of the British Commonwealth when they visited Edmonton in 1939. Pawel also met more visitors from Penticton and talked to them about the legendary *Ogopogo,* who supposedly lived in Okanagan Lake, and because of serpentine-like creature, tourists flocked to the *Peach City* each summer.

During the war, farmers like the Kowalchuk's have provided an essential service and were exempt from conscription. Everyone did what they could to help the war effort. Long into the night Evdokia knit woolen socks for Pawel and with Roman saved, anything that needed to be recycled.
Old bones were collected and melted down for fat and glue.

Fat from cooking was saved in tins on top of the warming oven of the wood stove and along with the fat from the bones, made glycerin that was turned into high explosives.

The Kowalchuk's also saved scrap metal, old pots, tin cans, coat hangers and balls of silver paper. All were required by the Canadian government for one purpose or another. Later there were ration books, which determined what rationed food one could buy. Farmers were able to grow their own food but one item of great importance was sugar for canning and baking.

During 1940 another provincial election was held. Social Credit and its candidate, Alphonse Mussault, won the riding of Bonnyville. Again the election was hotly contested on racial grounds – French vs Ukrainian but prosperity began and the Depression was over.
On December 7, 1941, without warning, Japanese war bombed Pearl Harbor. United States, which had remained isolationist, was stunned by the terrible losses and declared war on Japan the following day.

Paul White's prediction two decades earlier was on target. Japan not only bombed Pearl Harbor but also the Philippines, Wake and Guam islands.

When this happened, World War 11 was well underway and Japanese-speaking Canadians living on the West Coast of British Columbia had their property confiscated for fear they would help Japan.

By 1942 Japanese-Canadians were interned into the interior part of the province and other parts of Western Canada after a Japanese submarine lobbed two shells in the general direction of the Estavan Point Lighthouse in Vancouver. The date was June 20, 1942. The submarine submerged hurriedly with the record of having launched the first enemy attack on Canada since the Americans did in the war of 1812.

# CHAPTER FIFTEEN

During 1943 as the war progressed, Pawel Kowalchuk, Walter Barba and Marcel Gateau were members of the Loyal Edmonton Regiment of the First Canadian Infantry division in a battle against Hitler's *Nazi Supermen* in Ortona, Italy. It was one of the Second World War's most savage combats.
A letter from Pawel was always welcome. In one from the battlefront to Gloria, he in part wrote:

Dear Gloria,

It's rough day and night. Fighting never seems to stop. Ortona, perched above the Adriatic Sea of Italy's east coast was founded by the Trojans after Troy fell to the Ancient Greeks about 3200 years ago.

As I'm writing this letter its Christmas week and Ortona is a hell of deafening noise and splitting steel.

The more merciless the battle the harder both sides are fighting from window to window, from door to door. It's a carnival fury of tears, sweat and blood.

The Germans are using every trick imaginable including mines and flamethrowers.

I miss everyone back home, especially you Gloria and the twins. The way you describe Joe and Moe in your last letter they must be fun to be with. Are they taking boxing lessons?

I've got to pick up my gun and go back to work.

Pass on the word that Marcel Gateau and Walter Barba will be writing soon.

During that week the soldiers from Edmonton and Northern Alberta spearheaded an assault on Orotona in a battle as heroic as in the legend of the Greek poet, Homer.

The siege took ten days. Having marched north up the spine of Italy for five months the Loyal Eddies used as assault or shock troops had already fought one of Germany's elite combat units such as the Woffen SS and the 90th Panzer Division. But Ortona was Eddie's first big battle of the war and where it suffered most casualties.

The Canadian soldiers faced the German combat units, the Fallshirmaeger, the first German parachute division

The paratroopers were all volunteers, big, reckless, and highly trained with a reputation for toughness, boldness and bravery. But when it came to bravery so were the Royal Eddies. The Germans placed demolitions to funnel out the Eddies into Ortona's main street, which was picked as the *killing ground.*

Every street in Ortona had murderous crossfire and was booby-trapped. Piles of rubble from destroyed buildings were covered with mines.

When Canadians turned on their radios they heard a CBC war correspondent described Ortona this way, "There's street fighting everywhere. Private Pawel Kowalchuk of Bonnyville, Alberta killed six German paratroopers single handed and his brother in law, Marcel Gateau, killed fourteen."

In a subsequent report the correspondent report that the Germans mined a house and retreated. I heard a boom and soon discovered that privates Marcel Gateau and Walter Barba both from Bonnyville, Alberta, were inside and killed."

The announcement brought Roman closer to the radio and to Evdokia who had turned up the volume, said, "Anyone who talks about how nice war is, even if one improves the economy, is a fool."

What Gloria, her parents, Nick and Olga Barba said, was something similar. They couldn't believe their sons and a brother were dead but maybe wounded. And then there was a telegram confirming the deaths and that the bodies would be returned to Bonnyville for burial.

A week later, it was an emotional scene when Father Lapointe at the St. Louis Catholic Church said a mass for the deceased and in the process blessed Marcel and Walter's casket with holy water. The two caskets were placed in front of the altar but unopened because as Father Lapointe said earlier, "The remains are unrecognizable."

The Gateau's, Barba's and Kowalchuk's sat in the front row. There wasn't a dry eye in the entire church when the parish priest said, "Blessed are the names of Marcel Gateau and Walter Barba who have given up their lives for Canada. May the war end soon and their soul enter heaven."

# CHAPTER SIXTEEN

By the time Ortona was captured by the Allies in 1944 Kwitka graduated as a teacher but chose an entertainment career instead.
The rags to riches tale of Kwitka began by first singing at weddings and funerals and then at grungy water hole in Bonnyville where she accompanied herself on the guitar and a harmonica. Kwitka continued to cross east central Alberta with stops in St. Paul, Lloydminster and Vermilion. When she reached Edmonton she sang in front of a butcher shop in the city's farmers' market and earned her first one-hundred dollars. The gig in Calgary was unfortunately cancelled because there was anger among Calgaryians that Edmonton was still the capital of Alberta and not *Cow Town*.

Next, Kwitka left Edmonton and spent many of her adventuress trips by entertaining troops at various Canadian military camps. Since there were no telephones in many rural parts of Alberta at the time, Kwitka tried to come home as often as she could.

It was during one visit that Kwitka dressed in charcoal gray suit and hair smoothed back and pinned up, leaving her forehead and neck clean and bare as pride itself sat confidently across the table drinking tea with her mother and said, "My intention is go to New York and find myself an agent."

Further into the chitchat Kwitka said, "I'm using the name *Kwitka* because the word in Ukrainian mans a flower."

Evdokia responded with, "I know what the word *Kwitka* means but the pictures you sent last month were terrible."

"What's wrong with the picture?"

"The apparel you are wearing is skimpy; you are exposing your cleavage, and take a look at your bleached blond hair. I haven't seen many blond Ukrainian women."

"Mom, that's the style. Watch as soon as the war is over women will be changing hairstyle and fashions and even smoking cigars."

Kwitka and her mother promised each other not to discuss Kwitka's son born out of wedlock and given up for adoption.

This suited Kwitka just fine because she had other things to discuss and one was her attitude toward her Catholic faith.

"Catholicism gives me inner strength and I haven't rejected it yet but on the other hand I don't attend mass any more, if that makes sense, but I believe in a super power."

Evdokia then asked her daughter what she thought about dying.

"Well, I don't believe in an afterlife, though I'm not completely certain there isn't one either. There is something up there; some unexplained energy but I don't know what it is."

Then Evdokia asked if personally Kwitka was afraid of dying.

"I'm not afraid of anything."

Amazed, Evdokia said, "If Sister Raphael heard you speak that way she would…"

Kwitka interrupted, "Hey, Mom, I also don't go to confession, recite the rosary or make Stations of the Cross any more but doing things together appeals to me"

She had a sip of her tea and continued, "As for Sister Raphael, I thought you knew."

"Knew, what?"

"She is no longer the principal ad Bonnyville High School. And do you want to know something else?"

"I'm listening."

"Sister Raphael has left the Catholic Church and has married the Jew, Abe Goldman. They are presently living in San Francisco and operate the Arc Angel Night Club. Someday I hope to perform there."

"Oh, mother of Jesus!" Evdokia exclaimed.

"Because of the war, how rapidly things are changing."

"I'm glad you noticed, Mom. And you better learn to adapt to the changes that are still to come."

Changes like what?"

"Television and the computer will revolutionize world communication."

Evdokia really wanted to be part of a change but didn't know how. Being a decision maker however, she said, "Okay Kwitka, I'll try." Kwitka was of the opinion that no matter how things change, a person's response may be same so she said, "Mom, how?"

"I'll try to convince Dad to leave Bonnyville and buy a vineyard in British Columbia."

"That's a significant decision."

"Accompanied by heartaches perhaps," Evdokia said and left it at that

# CHAPTER SEVENTEEN

During the month of May, 1945 the Loyal Edmonton Regiment was preparing to attack the Dutch town of Amersfoort but orders came to stand firm as a truce between Germany and the Allies was about to be signed. Several days later there was dancing on the streets of Bonnyville and the world as VE Day was announced. It would take time to heal the wounds but the memories of Hitler would never be erased.

It was a time when Pawel was discharged from military service and returned to Bonnyville but not before he stopped in New York and visited Kwitka who had hired an agent and was performing at a nightclub off Broadway.

While on his way home from the war, Pawel spent several days in New York and both discussed a deal that once his dream hotel was built, she would participate at the official opening ceremonies.

Along the way Pawel also stopped in Winnipeg and met with Peter Black and Paul White who gave him a tour of the Mancan operations which they owned.
The war with Japan still continued but military experts said it wouldn't last long, and it didn't. On the day Pawel reached Bonnyville, he, his hometown and the world celebrated again. It was Victory over Japan day.

As soon as Japan surrendered to the Allies World War 11 was officially over and Canadians and the entire world celebrated again. It was a time when economic growth produced an abundance of consumer goods and the horse, still a common means of transportation disappeared and railways had been largely displaced as means of travel by automobiles and aircraft.

It was in 1946 that Evdokia received a long awaited letter from her nephew Bogdan, from Lviv, Ukraine.

As part of the World War 11 settlement eastern part of Poland including the city of Lvov, whose name was changed to Lviv, was handed to the Soviet Union and eastern part of Germany to Poland. Evdokia with her big brown and intrepid eyes opened it. In part the letter read:

Dear aunt Evdokia,

With regard to your query about my mother I, sadly write that she did not survive the Ukraine famine. Until recently seven-million Ukrainians were starved to death and my mother was one of them as she was exiled to Kazakhstan for writing articles that the Kulaks were being liquidated as a class because they endangered the success of Communism.

History books of the world will not ignore the great crime of genocide against the Ukraine people. It appears Stalin used the famine as a political weapon to destroy Ukrainian aspirations for Independence. At the same time as the famine (1932 – 1934) a wave of persecutions of thousands of Ukraine intellectuals, writers, and leaders took place; many deported to Siberia and forced to work in labor camps. I was one of the labor camp victims until recently.  Please understand why I could not acknowledge your letter.

My mother, like Bishop Budka last year, was arrested and exiled for reporting the truth. For this the Communists left my Mom, like they did with Bishop Budka after he returned to Lvov from Canada in 1927 and served as Vicar General of the Metropolitan Curia until 1945. My Mom was sent to a prison camp in Kazakhstan where she died and her lifeless body left in the forest for wild animals to eat. By the way, Bishop Budka has been exiled to Siberia and living in a dismal barrack. Please pray for him as he is extremely weak and my not survive another year."
Your nephew Bogdan – Lviv, Ukraine – 1946

After reading the letter Evdokia cried and fainted. Her lips turned white, her arms outstretched.  For a moment she was death-like, but after recovering but weeping, she was concerned not only about her sister Filipa, Bishop Budka, and the famine in Ukraine but also her own identity as

mechanization was making rapid progress, so was science and technology.
There were discoveries in all walks of life including search for new sources of energy. There were minor wars and monarchs replaced. But it wasn't until 1947 that Canadians began with a new identity.

# CHAPTER EIGHTEEN

Under the Citizenship Act which came into effect January 1, immigrants were no longer *British Subjects* but first and foremost Canadian Citizens, soon to be issued with their own passports and served by their own embassies abroad. By now Canadians were settling back to normal life after six years of global conflict. 1947 was the last of more than a million Canadian soldiers; sailors and airmen had been brought back home leaving 42,000 comrades in cemeteries across Europe and Asia.

By law, any veteran wanting his old job back could have it. But thousands accepted government grants to establish their own businesses or farms, purchase new tools or equipment or get more education. Canada's population was 12.5 million and growing fast.

For each new baby, a mother received a family allowance cheque of $5.00 a month, a measure introduced during the war.

In mid-1947 unemployment in Canada was only 1.6 percent and the average weekly wage was $36.00 and many earned more than that. After years of war-torn restraint Canadians were ready for a spending spree. Since Roman and Evdokia had money to splurge and believed that mixed farming in east central Alberta was the lowest occupation one could have, they sold their farm to Jacques and Yvette Gateau, traveled to British Columbia and purchased the Purple Grape Vineyard in Penticton from Ed Ami's parents who wished to retire and live in Arizona. The vineyard had a commanding view of Okanagan Lake and the mountains behind it and a short distance from where Pawel had purchased lakeshore property while he and Gloria were on their honeymoon. When Roman and Evdokia returned to Bonnyville they got rid of their machinery, tools and furniture by holding an auction sale. The livestock was sold to an agent for Edmonton Stockyards. Evdokia's piano was shipped to Penticton.

1947 was a time when Department store sales soared. Eaton's advertised women's spring coats for $14.95 and a new electric washing machine with a wringer for $82.00, a pack of cigarettes would cost one 35 cents and a gallon of gasoline thirty-four. Cars? A Cadillac would most one more that $3000 but the basic Chevy, Ford and Plymouth for less than $1500.  Average cost of a house was $6000 and while it was small, boxlike structures, they were better than doubling up with an in-law.

In the dance halls Canadians were tapping feet to a new Latin American rhythm, the samba. Frank Sinatra and Bing Crosby were crooning and wooing young girls' hearts with songs like *Near You, The Anniversary Song, Oh, How We Danced On The Night We Were Wed* and *How are things In Glocca Morra?* But the real hit of the year was a screwball song by Kwitka entitled, *Call it Stormy Monday But Tuesday is Just as Bad*.

The movie theatres were showing classics as *Great Expectations, Life with Father, Odd Man Out* and *Farmer's Daughter*.
And Canadians listened and danced to the music of Bert Niosi, Art Hallman and Mart Kenny and his Western Gentlemen.
Television was still five years away and radio

was still king with many programs originating in United States: Jack Benny, Fibber McGee and Molly, Lux Radio Theatre among others. From the CBC came such programs as John and Judy, The Jackson's, Citizen Forum, and Just Mary.

When it came to sports, Saturday night stay-at-homers could tune into Foster Hewitt describing Maple Leaf games and Maurice Richard of the Montreal Canadiens and Barbara Scott who won the ladies world skating championships, became national heroes. Josiah Alexander was delighted when he heard that Jackie Robinson, batting champion with the Montreal Royals of the International League, the previous year, made history by becoming the first Black player to be signed up for Big League baseball, starting the season at first base with the Brooklyn Dodgers.

On the economic front, the discovery of oil and natural gas at Leduc on February 13, 1947, was followed by uncovering other fields in Alberta including one on the Kowalchuk farm that was recently sold to

Jacques Gateau. Jacques didn't have the mineral rights but did well financially as the oil company kept paying for the right to trespass the land in order to serve the oil wells and a pipe line it had built.

On the world scene attempts to get the Soviet Union to agree to a peace treaty for Germany and Austria failed. Stalin had also reneged on his pledge to hold free elections in the Eastern European countries as Roman had predicted and the famine to starve Ukrainians continued.

These countries were solidly under Communist domination as Churchill put it at Fulton, Mo on March 5, 1946, "From Stettin in the Baltic to Trieste in the Adriatic, an iron curtain has descended across the continent." Events elsewhere were also shaping the postwar world – Britain granted India its independence, which caused bloody clashes between Hindus and Muslims, including a three-day orgy of hatred in Calcutta that left 5000 dead. Britain had also decided to rid itself of another troublesome thorn, the conflicting land claims and aspirations of

Arab and Jew in her terrorist-hidden Palestine module.

Politics and war apart, 1947 was eventful in many ways. A Bedouin boy exploring a cave in northwest Palestine's Dead Sea discovered some ancient scrolls of parchment. They contained all but two parts of the *Old Testament* book of Isaiah. One of the happiest events of 1947 wasn't that Roman and Evdokia became citizens of Penticton or the marriage, on November 22 of Princess Elizabeth and Lieut. Philip Mountbatten of the Royal Navy but that Kwitka's *I Left My Love in Canada* was number one on *Billboards Top Tem* parade of hits.

# CHAPTER NINETEEN

During 1948 Pawel and Gloria followed the senior Kowalchuk's to Penticton, British Columbia and settled in a three-bedroom apartment of Scott Street. As soon the family, including teenagers Moe and Joe were settled in; Pawel obtained a license and became a realtor. He had lost interest in Aberhart, Social Credit and politics generally. Pawel gained employment with Okanagan Realty Ltd. managed by Don Ferguson, a knowledgeable agent who enjoyed Powel's friendship and because of a hot market, the commissions he earned for the company. Gloria meanwhile, gained employment at the Penticton General Hospital as an operating nurse.

Things went smoothly for both until 1956 when Pawel's dream to build a hotel on the southern shore of Okanagan Lake was taking shape. He spoke about the multi-million dollar project so often that many a day Gloria became embarrassed if not annoyed.

The pressure for Pawel to succeed and have his passionate dream come true was so overwhelming that he spoke on the subject to anyone who cared to listen. His favorite sayings were: "Where there's a will there's a way." and, "Imagination is just as important as knowledge."

These were only expressions but according to Pawel the inn would be built by the end of 1957 and make Penticton a favorite resort city.

"You even talk about the hotel in your sleep," Gloria protested as Pawel continued to fantasize what a beautiful hotel it was going to be. Pawel was surprised, however, on one September morning, when he woke up, that Gloria, an environment freak and her serotonin level must have been down, as she screamed at him, "Like hell, are you going to build a hotel along the shore of the pristine Okanagan Lake! And I'm not finished. I'll do everything in my power, you don't. Penticton doesn't need another hotel but more beaches so residents can enjoy themselves." Pawel was devastated by the sudden rebuff and Gloria only made matters worse with her continuous chatter.

"And do you want something else?" she said. Pawel was not offended nor did he feel superior when he said, "What?"

"There are those in Penticton who feel the same way as I do."

"I understand, not many."

"But there are."

"Name one."

"Ed Ami, the principal at Penticton High School."

"That goof. His head still isn't screwed on right."

Ed Ami, a principle at Penticton High School since 1936 and in that time had not married. Although he had aged since leaving Bonnyville there were no wrinkles on his face.

At the Elite Restaurant Ami was having a cup of coffee and reading the *Herald* newspaper when he flipped several pages and came to a section marked *Today in History 1956.* He read the article with interest, "Nineteen years ago today the marriage of Gloria Gateau and Pawel Kowalchuk took place in Bonnyville, Alberta.

It was the first wedding in east central part of Alberta that a French Canadian woman married a Ukrainian gentlemen…"

Ami's curiosity was aroused because while he was a vice-principal in Bonnyville, Gloria was one of his star pupils that he wanted to date.

Ami also recalled, as flashes raced through his mind, how Pawel was expelled from his school after Ami caught him and Gloria sharing a bottle of chokecherry wine during a Sadie Hawkins Halloween dance. And he also recalled how Pawel defeated him in a political race and later became Gloria's husband.

The wedding was reported locally in the *Bonnyville Nouvelle* and the *Canadian Press* newsgathering agency that has bureaus throughout Canada.

Ami glanced at his watch. The time was 8:00 a. m.

"I'm going to get even with Pawel Kowalchuk for the way he humiliated me and then married Gloria," Ami thought and went on rationalizing, "Gloria is opposed to the construction of a hotel Pawel is proposing. I'm going to exploit his and Gloria's differences to the limit."

After enjoying his coffee Ami headed to his office and when he reached it, said to his secretary, Monica Woodstock, "Good morning Monica, What have I got this morning?'

Ami had already s spotted a two-foot high lettered *Principal Ami* Sucks sign painted in bold red on the side of the brick and stone wall of the high school. Harry, the custodian, had already informed him of the sign and also of a break-in.

"Did security call police?"

"Harry did," Ami replied and went on, "Whoever did it also broke a window, crawled through it and then broke into several lockers. Now for today, what else have I got to deal with?"

"Mrs. Gomez, that's Jose's mother, is irate for having her son suspended and will be in to see you," Monica said and while glancing at her date book continued, "Mr. Feddo, the drama teacher, wants the auditorium for a rehearsal, and the painter wants a decision on the color you want to paint the hallway."

Monica paused a second. "Oh yes, aside from school work don't forget the meeting scheduled about the hotel that is proposed by Pawel Kowalchuk."

In the background a radio station interrupted its regular programming with a late breaking news item: "Negotiations between the Penticton School Board and its teachers' has broken off. There's concern about the possibility of a strike. Teachers are demanding a five percent wage increase but the School Board says it can't afford it. Some teachers are saying they are planning work-to-rule. Stay tuned for more Okanagan news. Now back to our music. Here is Kwitka to sing *Ave Maria*."

Ami glanced at his watch, left for the office, as it was now 8:25 a. m. and greeted staff and students alike as they began filling the hallways. Some of the greetings were acknowledged while others weren't. Many of the students were still yawning.

While in the hallway the grade eleven teacher invited Ami to a Roman lunch with poetry reading, which was accepted.

"Thank you for the invitation. "I'll enjoy that." Ami said.

By 8:55 teachers and students were in their respective rooms and Ami spoke to them on the public address system.

"Good morning everyone, staff and students. I trust many of you have noticed the graffiti on the side of the school. If any student from Pen High was involved, you have until 2:30 to own up and see me in my office. Any student having any information regarding the B and E please let me know."

There was shuffling of paper in each classroom.

"Now for the good news," Ami continued. "Over the weekend, in basketball, the Lakers won 88-82 against the Kamloops Chiefs while the Lakettes lost in a tournament in Kelowna. The music class sold two-hundred boxes of chocolates and Joe and Moe Kowalchuk won their boxing matches at a tournament in Vancouver. To the winners and losers, congratulations."

Joe Kowalchuk was a typical 16-year-old teenager extricating himself from difficult situations and with the special cunning with which young boys are gifted. In fact he wasn't a model boy but loved participating in outdoor sports. No matter what scrapes he got into, what punishment he received, he bore no malice. His memory was short.

Moe on the other hand was a teenager that was constantly in a state of rebellion against authority. He called police *pigs* and *fuzz* and enjoyed a new phenomenon, rock n roll music, particularly when Kwitka sang Bill Haley, Little Richard, Chuck Berry and Elvis Presley tunes. Moe was also the envy of other boys because of his absolute freedom from paternal control.

Both teenagers were small for their age and wiry, and despite their stature enjoyed boxing most of all the sports.

When Ami returned to his office the vice-principal, Hugh Smith, was already waiting.

"Anything more about the break-in?" Smith asked as soon as Ami sat at his desk and began drinking a cup of coffee.

"I have. Aside from the graffiti, damage to student lockers someone stole a jock strap from the coach's locker."

Next Smith brought up the subject of the Sadie Hawkins Halloween dance.

"Why don't we get the *Herald* to cover it," Ami said.

"Publicity isn't the problem. It's the coats. Where are we going to put the coats?"

"What's the problem with the coats?"

"The gym is sealed off from the rest of the school and the students do not have access to the lockers.

"In order to dance they have to remove their coats and we have to find a place for them. Is that the idea?"

"Yes."

Ami then asked, "How many kids are we expecting?"

"About five-hundred."

Puzzled, Ami said, "I still don't get it. What's with the coats removed?

"To be candid, to eliminate the chance students hiding booze and drugs under their coats.

Last year if you recall, there was an enterprising kid by the name of Sobo Birch who smuggled in a bottle of wine and when he consumed it, thought he was paddling a canoe trying to find Ogopogo in Okanagan Lake."

Ami was anxious what was on the label of the wine bottle."

"The bottle had no label but by the shape one could tell it was *Pride Of the Okanagan – Vintage 1918.*

"Anything else?"

"Music students during the weekend chocolate blitz sold another two-hundred chocolate boxes in order to buy a bus."

The same morning, five blocks away, Pawel attended a weekly sales meeting at Okanagan Realty where he was employed as a salesman. Pawel was a salesman who never took rejection as a personal matter and among other things having experience as a politician, thought of himself as an exceptionally talented realtor. He studied real estate market trends, drew various graphs and maps, was persistent and had confidence in his ability to do what he wanted to do most – negotiate deals and own a hotel in Penticton.

Pawel had talent and craftsmanship and each morning while driving on his way to work listened to motivational tapes.

He worked twelve hours a day, tried to contact as many vendors and purchasers as he could, carried an electronic pager and had a radiophone in his car.

Grabbing a cup of coffee the salesmen then sat in their bull pens and with Don Ferguson, the sales manage, discussed listings taken and sales made during the weekend.  Among other topics discussed were Open Houses held, advertising, collapsed deals and Commercial Properties that were available.

It was while discussing Commercial Properties that Pawel stood up and outlined his architectural plan for a twelve-story, 200-room hotel on the shore of Okanagan Lake. It was felt by some however, that a hotel of that magnitude would interfere with the environments in one way or another.

Some felt the beach property was more suited for a museum, there would be traffic congestion and because of the height planes have difficulty to land at the nearby airport. Still others were against progress of any kind, period.

"What hurts most," Pawel said about the $75-million project is that my wife, Gloria, along with Ed Ami, principal at the Penticton High School, are vehemently opposed to construction of the hotel."

"If I had a wife like that I would divorce her," one of the salesmen said.

Because of his strict upbringing Pawel was against divorce and abortion.

When Ferguson asked about the construction time-period Pawel said, "It should begin December 1 of this year and according to plans, rezoning approved, the official opening will take place before 1958."

Before a tour of the new listing was to begin, Ferguson called Pawel into his office and in a soft voice said, "What is this I hear about you and Gloria?"

"I'd rather not discuss it, the situation is tense."

"You should talk about the relationship. My experience is that what bothers you at home also bothers you at work. Is it because of Ed Ami?"

Pawel said that it was and Gloria had asked Ed for a divorce.

"I figured as much. Hang in there. Do your utmost to get City Council approve the zoning? Eventually it will be rewarding not only to you personally but also to the city of Penticton."

As Pawel was making his exit Ferguson grabbed his hand and at the same time said, "Say hello to your sons, they need encouragement at a time when a family is disintegrating."

"I will, I love Joe and Moe dearly."

After Pawel did a tour of the new listings he returned to his desk and placed several phone calls. First, he spoke with Mayor David Edwards whom he helped to get reelected in the last municipal election. But the most important call Pawel made was to call someone he could surround himself with and trust, Paul Black and Peter White, in Winnipeg, who's *Mancan* Corporation was now listed in *Fortune* magazine. Pawel had to convince his relatives that Penticton was good investment territory.

At first Mr. Black was reluctant but after discussing the subject with his partner, White to co-invest with Pawel he said, "Pardon me if I sound a little suspicions, I don't want to waste your time or mine until I know that the property you speak of is appraised and zoned."

Pawel did not appear upset by his uncle's concern, quite the contrary, "I must admit your analysis of the situation in Penticton is the correct one. Mayor Edwards, however, has assured me city council will ram the zoning through, as there seems to be a lot of support for the project, particularly from the Chamber of Commerce."

"If that is the truth, then I'll agree in principle to have our company, *Mancan.* Co-venture the project.

"You'll never regret this venture. We'll even name the hotel he *Lakeshore Mancan Inn* in honor your company."

White appreciated the gesture and said that as soon as the zoning for the beach property was approved, he and his wife Erin, would fly to Penticton.

The meeting at the Penticton High School gym started on time with Gloria and Ami sitting side by side at the head table acting as chairpersons.

"We are here tonight simply as a voice against construction of a hotel that my husband is proposing," Gloria began to an audience of one hundred. "We feel the beech property in question should be kept in its natural state or made into a public park."

Ami took over, "And we are not against free enterprise but hope one realizes once city council approves zoning, a hotel of such proportions will block the view of many residents, particularly those living on Main and Martin streets." Ami paused for a second. "We want to join those who feel there already is an over-abundance of hotels, motels and guest homes in Penticton, as it is."

Ami then took out a sheet of paper from his valise and pointing to vacancy rates in each hotel and motel went on, "Hotels and motels in Penticton are having a difficult time as it is. We believe City Council should have better control of lakefront property development." Ami hesitated while having a drink of water from a glass placed in front of him.

"We understand City Council is about to sign an intent-agreement, permitting the hotel co ventured by Pawel Kowalchuk and the giant Mancan Corporation from Winnipeg and that Mr. Kowalchuk wants approval as soon as possible. Well, if that is the case those opposed to the project will have to demonstrate making certain approval isn't granted."

Next, Ami leaned towards Gloria and tested the audience's reaction. He got several responses when he directed a question at no one in particular, "What do you think?"

A Salvation Army captain who identified himself as Reginald Stone, walked up to the microphone that was conveniently placed on the middle of the floor, and said, "I must categorically say that my congregation is opposed to the construction because of the traffic congestion that will affect our Sunday service"

Mr. Stone's second objection was," The garbage that will be strewn all over."

If any of these arguments swayed Pawel he didn't show it, then after approaching the microphone, after several other objectors had spoken, talked at length in favor of the development and its multi uses and attracting tourists.

"Our study shows that Penticton can't continually turn down commercial development and furthermore, when the hotel is completed it will provide employment for at least one-hundred people," he began and ended with, 'A museum on the site can't be built because I own the land."

Gloria appeared irritated and after calling for suggestions on how to stop the project, and if it wasn't, to hold a public protest demonstration.

The meeting lasted one-hour and after views and ideas were suggested, the demonstration date was set for the first Sunday following Halloween.

As everyone was leaving the gymnasium Pawel overheard Ami say to Gloria, "Friend, let's go and have a drink."

Gloria obliged and the couple spent time together at the Three Gables Bar until past midnight.

Gloria staggered home at 12:30 a. m., a time when Joe and Moe were sleeping. Pawel was still sitting in the living room studying blueprints when Gloria strolled next to him leaned over and said, "Pawel, you made a fool out of yourself this evening.

Now you must realize that a lot of people in Penticton believe there should be no hotel on the site you are proposing. The inn would eliminate a large portion of a sandy beach and ducks, Canada geese and trumpeter swans will have no place to go during winter."

For a moment Pawel felt sad because earlier in the evening he had a conversation with Mayor Edwards who told him that City Council had postponed the zoning hearing. A delegation from Greenpeace and another by Captain Stone of the Salvation Army and backed by Ami and Gloria, had signed a three-hundred-name petition protesting construction of the inn vehemently.

After an intense argument Gloria became ballistic and said, "Pawel dear, we are so far apart with our goals in life that I suggest we separate.

My father always had said that I shouldn't have married someone with a different heritage. Our marriage has been going belly up ever since we moved to Penticton."

"And it's no coincidence that while I was in Winnipeg arranging financing for the project that Ed Ami stepped in your life," Pawel said and went on, "Look, if it's a diversion that you want instead of demonstrating and parading, why don't you check on the Acme Record Store where Joe and Moe purchase their rock n roll albums?"

"Rock n roll is a disgrace especially the way Kwitka sings it," Gloria said and then imitated Kwitka in a derogatory way. After still more arguing and sobbing Gloria said, "Pawel, since you began preoccupying yourself with the hotel, you have changed, you aren't the same person who I married in Bonnyville. And I realize you won't give me a divorce so a separation is the next best thing."

"Hand me a sponge so I can wipe your tears," Pawel replied as his mind for a second returned to the moment of vow- taking during their wedding when Father Lapointe said at the time, 'What God has joined, men and women must not divide.' "There are two children involved and who moves out."

"I'll move out. And Joe and Moe can live with me." Gloria said.

"And the three of you will live with Ami?

"I guess so."

"Are you guessing or are you definite?"

"I'm definite."

"Of course you realize a separation will disrupt the family unit. You mean the absolute world to me so why don't you just cool it and try to salvage our marriage?"

Gloria would have nothing to do saving hers.

"We'll divide everything equally, fifty-fifty," Gloria continued.

"Like a chattel, we are going to divide each child. You take an arm and I take a leg?"

"I'm certain Joe and Moe are old enough to which parent they want to live with"

"And so that's it, a separation. No fanfare. For a boy who could recite the Hail Mary before I could walk, it's hard to take."

"I'm sorry it had to happen this way but knowing you, you'll find someone else to love."

A tear formed on Pawel's cheek. Never in his entire life had he been so humiliated as he was during the past five minutes.

Gloria continued, "And it's not my midlife crises or an early menopause. I just I can't understand why you want to build a hotel on a beautiful beech, that will be twelve stories high?"

Pawel and Gloria were locked in a battle over a marriage that began as a fairytale and ending in acrimony. That night Gloria went to sleep in a bed downstairs but not before she slammed the living room door in Pawel's face.

As Pawel went to sleep in a separate bed that night he had difficulty sleeping. All the good times he shared with Gloria raced through his mind. That same night, however, he had a dream, not about the hotel he was building but about Gloria in Ami's arms.

The Purple Grape Vineyard looked like most other vineyards in the Okanagan valley although the house on the ten-acre parcel of land was modern compared to the log one the Kowalchuk's lived in near Bonnyville.

Pawel had stopped to visit his parents and said to both over a cup of coffee, "Gloria and I have finally separated."

Evdokia raised her eyebrows, "See, I told you French women aren't like Ukrainian and that your marriage wouldn't last."

"Well, nineteen years of marriage isn't that bad these days," Roman said. "But who's taking care of Joe and Moe?"

"Gloria is but hopefully that will change."

"When?

"As soon as the Lakeshore Mancan Inn is built."

"That may take years."

"No, Dad, one year the most."

Pawel and his parents talked for fifteen minutes before he made an exit and Evdokia revealed a long hidden talent for playing the piano. She had studied music for five years at a Lvov orphanage, and still had the touch. Her favorite composers were Shevchenko, Dankevych and Gubarenko.

The following evening, Pawel was back following an invitation for supper – roast beef, mashed potatoes, green peas, baby carrots, ice cream and all the wine one could drink.

This time Pawel and his parents did not discuss the Lakeshore Mancan Inn or his separation from Gloria. They sat at a kitchen table enjoying Roman's wine and talked about how much better is was to grow grapes instead of wheat, the Septober Wine Festival and how rapidly their lives were changing because of technology that continued to catch one's imagination.

"Television has replaced the radio as a form of entertainment. And Kwitka has already seen hundreds simulated murders before appearing on the *Ed Sullivan Show,*" Evdokia said.

"And IBM has computers that are smarter than people. Who knows? We may soon see an astronaut on the moon?" Roman continued. Then Pawel mentioned the gradual disappearance of farm workhorses and grain elevators and the appearance of combines, fancy cars and jets.

Next Pawel talked about farmers who were beginning the process of urbanization and that the major battles of the 21st century would be fought in cyberspace. What Pawel said was on target. True no one died of AIDS yet but parents worried about polio, whooping cough and tuberculosis.

A university education was a privilege and not a right. There was global warming, a Cold War and plenty of emotional and physical scars left over from World War 11.

"And there was no *pill* and a tubal legation was difficult to obtain," Roman continued. Evdokia turned to Roman, who was sitting beside him in an attitude of patient dejection but at that moment Roman rose, and after stretching his stiffened legs she said,

"As far as I'm concerned every new parent in Canada today should get down on bended knees and thank God for modern miracles, especially the disposable diaper."

After discussing Pawel's doubts, concerns and worries about his family situation, Roman said, "Pawel, your marital situation is nothing to be ashamed of. Statistics show that one out of twelve marriages in Canada end up in divorce. Do you need psychological help to cope with your and Gloria's separation?"

Pawel said he didn't and looked upon psychiatrists as "Useless Shrinks." It was at this point that Pawel thought he should speak to the parish priest, Father Julian Cook, instead and left the living room, picked up the telephone receiver, dialed a number, which led to an appointment.

On Friday morning Ami's school routine was basically the same – problem solving. The *Principal Ami Sucks* sign had been repainted, hallways were brighter in color and Ed Ami would co-chair another meeting of the anti-hotel committee. Monica, his secretary, reminded him of an appointment with an irate parent at ten and another with basketball coach at eleven.

Frustrated, Ami said about his appointments, "We surmount one problem, another pops up, Give advice, and lend a shoulder for the kids to cry on, talk to the parents, maybe get sued and make sure the building is still standing. Sometimes I feel like retiring."

Monica didn't want to discuss Ami's personal problems. Instead she said, "You are in a social pressure cooker, that's what it is. Despite the teacher-School Bard dispute, morale appears to be high at the school." Ami nodded his head signifying that it was. "Besides the two appointments what else is on the schedule?"

"The School Board has laid charges against the student who did the graffiti, broke a window and vandalized the lockers before a court date is set."

"Is the kid, Sobo Birch?"

"Regretfully it is."


Pawel had a free afternoon, of sorts. He intended to work on the Mancan Inn plans but reminded himself of an appointment he had made with Father Ryan. It wouldn't be the first time Pawel confessed to a priest. As a younger man he went to confession at least once a month and not like some of his Catholic friends only during Easter and Christmas. And the priest always gave him advice that was free.

This was different however; Pawl felt that during a confrontation with Gloria that he had not sinned.  Well, maybe there were several venial sins, but taken to the cleaners by Gloria, now his ex-wife.

Father Alexander Ryan, 50-year old priest had a voice that was resonant and deep and while in the rectory Pawel sat in front of his desk. The only advice Father Ryan gave that day was what Saint Francis of Assisi once said:

Lord, make me an instrument of your peace.
Where there is hatred, let me sow love;
Where there is injury, pardon;
Where there is doubt, faith;
Where there is despair, hope;
Where there is darkness, light;
And where there is sadness, joy.
O Divine master, grant that I may not so much seek
To be consoled as to console;
To be understood as to understand;
To be loved as to love.
For it is in giving that we receive;
It is in pardoning that we are pardoned;
And it is in dying that we are born to eternal life.

By the time Principal Ami talked with police and Sobo Birch's foster parent, Tina Kent, it was ten in the morning. Waiting for him in the hallway meanwhile, stood Erlinda Gomez. When Mrs. Gomez confronted Ami she was apologetic. Her son Jose was given a maximum suspension for remarks and a gesture he had made to a female in his English class. The teacher and several classmates witnessed the incident.

"I'm sorry," Mrs. Gomez began. "But Jose's suspension is far too long."

"It's the School Board's policy,' Ami replied and continued, "I just follow directions given me by the School Board."

Mrs. Gomez pleaded a second time, "Jose did not know what *screw* off meant. Even I was told the words men to remove a lid form a jar preserving fruit."

"At grade twelve Jose knows better."

"Well, if Jose can't come to school, I'll have to sue."

Visibly upset but keeping his temper under control Ami said, "Fine, madam. If that's the way you feel then I'll see you in court."

As soon as Mrs. Gomez left Ami met with the basketball coach, Albert Short,

"Ed," short out of breath began, "I guess I have to report that in our basketball game against Vernon last night three of our boys were caught smoking marijuana. Two of the players were actually smoking while a third had drawn a puff and threw it away."

"Well, what can I say? It could have been booze instead."

"And one of the players also claims that his watch was missing. No one admitted to the theft so I had the players searched."

"The entire team?"

"Yes, I had them remove their clothing including their under-shorts but no watch was found."

"Okay, stay on top of it. There may have to be suspensions. I'll deal with it on Monday. Right now we have to prepare for the Sadie Hawkins dance."

Midway during the noon recess Ami received a phone call from Gloria.

They discussed a number of personal things including that in Ami's home the stairwell had to be repaired, an upcoming hotel demonstration march from the Plaza Shopping Mall to City Hall, and then to the site where the Lakeshore Mancan Inn was to be built.

After that particular conversation Gloria asked, "How are things at the school today?"

"Aside from routine problems the biggest challenge is keeping up moral. It's difficult at times when the teachers are planning to strike for more pay."

Ami also mentioned how difficult he found his role as a stepparent to Joe and Moe. "Our living together has hit the boys' right between the eyes."

Gloria then suddenly said, "I have to run. There's another patient being wheeled into the operating room. Goodbye."

Before Ami hung up however, he asked Gloria, "How was the last operation?"

"The operation was fine but the patient I must regretfully say, died. Goodbye, I'll see you after work."

A short time later Principal Ed Ami said to himself, "The Sadie Hawkins dance is only hours away."

He took comfort that before the dance began he would have dinner with Gloria at Granny Bogner's, a restaurant famous for cooking up excellent meals.

# CHAPTER TWENTY

Monday morning, Principal Ami was greatly relieved when the Sadie Hawkins dance was over but when he saw a line-up of parents wanting to speak to him he knew something extraordinary had happened. First, Mrs. Philips and her daughter Shirley greeted him. The grade eleven student had been bullied at the dance and her nose broken.

"Shirley says three classmates beat her up because she was out with one of their boyfriends," Mrs. Philips said and went on, "Sometimes I wonder what goes on in this school. It happened on school grounds during a school activity and I want to tell you there are going to be a lot of concerned parents nine months from now."

Mrs. Phillips kept pacing the floor in Ami's office when he was going to interrupt her but she was quite a talker and couldn't.

"Shirley admits being at the party and that she was out with Sobo Birch who fell through the ceiling in the science room."

Ami was surprised when Mrs. Philips told him how her daughter and Sobo got into the attic. They entered the crawl space above the ceiling and as they began crawling along Sobo fell to the floor after the ceiling tile gave way under him.

"Leave it to me," Ami assured the irate mother. "I'll deal with it."

"And I want it reported to the police," Mrs. Philips went on as she made her exit.

Minutes later, the social studies teacher, Stump Dexter, called complaining about the heat in his room. As soon as Ami was finished speaking to Dexter Monica brought in the mail, "There's a letter from the school board," she said.

Of particular interest was a copy of a letter that dealt with the social studies teacher who had just called about the heat. Dexter distorted claims that during the Protestant reigns there was peace and prosperity while during the Catholic reigns there was drunkenness and atrocities. It was also alleged that Dexter questioned the number of Jews murdered during the Second World War doubting the authenticity of the number of deaths claimed.

The school board requested that Dexter modify his teaching content.

After reading the letter Ami got up from his desk and to Monica said, "That won't help in boosting the teachers' morale. I bet the Teacher's Association will support and appeal to the Board Reference committee if Dexter defies the request and the board fires him. I better speak to Dexter and see what's going on," Ami said and then turning to Monica continued, "I'm like a parish priest in a confessional. I listen; give absolution and then say the Lord be with you."

To Monica the comment came as a surprise because Ami basically was a nonreligious person although as a younger man, embraced the Catholic faith.

In another letter that Monica handed to Ami several students complained to the School Board about the basketball coach and the stripping incident.

"Well, a member of the basketball team reported a stolen watch," Ami said while pacing up and down and reading the letter at the same time.

The letter was from members of the basketball team and in part read: "If we break the law, we are taken to jail. All the coach gets is his wrists slapped. We were down to our underwear when the coach said, 'All the Way.' We believe it's embarrassing that a teacher should do that to us."

The letter went on to say the students complied with the request and an apology by coach, Short, wasn't sincere. The School Board wanted a written report on the incident.

Ami's final news was encouraging. It was the only good news he had that day. The music teacher, Frank Tarafski, called saying band rehearsals were going well and an additional five-hundred chocolate bars had been sold over the weekend. Tarafski wanted to know if an additional shipment could be ordered in time for the anti-hotel march and demonstration.

Following the regular Monday morning meeting, salesmen at Okanagan realty Ltd. hopped into their cars and toured listings of other realtors than their own, as part of the ritual of property familiarization.

The first home was listed at $100,000. The four-bedroom bungalow had 4800 square feet of space with a view of Skaha and Okanagan lakes. The home had a circular driveway with the landscape flourishing. The vendor was Judge Harris Klinkhamer and his wife, Joan. In the basement salesmen found a Doberman pinscher tied up in h furnace room. Pawel was upset when he saw the dog and wondered since the judge was so cruel to animals how could he give proper sentences to people. The salesmen then proceeded to a home on Norton Street, a depressed area of the city, and a "Bulldozer Special" aptly described the home that was advertised in newspapers. A lockbox key was used to enter because the occupants Crash London and Boomer Grimes, weren't home at the time. As soon as the salesmen walked inside they found the hallway stacked with empty beer cases. A pot of pork and beans was still on the stove in the kitchen. In the living room the ashtrays were full, a guitar leaned against a wall, and a marijuana plant decorated the window at just the right angle not to be seen from outside.

The decorating scheme in the living room was unusual in that girlie magazine centerfolds covered the bearing wall instead of conventional wallpaper. The master bedroom was unorthodox also though the suits hanging in the closet were of modern cut and neatly pressed. Two of the walls were painted black. On the ceiling was a 3X 3 foot angled mirror. On a table below were a radio, a butcher knife, a revolver and a police scanner. While leaving the home Pawel said, "I wouldn't' be surprised if criminals lived here."

Next, Pawel drove to half-duplex on Government Street. While entering the living room one could immediately sense a widow was in mourning. Her husband's picture was hanging on the wall so that it was the main focus of attention. George Kent, Mrs. Kent said, was killed two weeks earlier while helping build a power line near Okanagan Lake.

Next to the picture hung a photograph of Sobo Birch, a foster child that was the same age as Joe and Moe.

When Pawel made a comment about the youths photograph Tina Kent sadly said, "Sobo will be leaving me soon because I'm a widow now. The way Sobo was treated before we took him in is a wonder he hadn't committed suicide."

Pawel did not pursue the matter but complimented Mrs. Kent for keeping her residence clean despite losing a husband followed by a foster child who was in continual trouble.

The final property the salesmen toured was acreage with a two-story home occupied by the Dr. Harjit Singh family that had emigrated from India. As the salesmen were milling about Dr. Singh appeared on the scene and seemed more concerned about the Penticton Sikh community than the condition of his home and dilapidated barn.

A conversation with Dr. Singh was cut short however, when his electronic pager sounded. "Excuse me," he apologized. "I'm on call and an ambulance is on its way to the hospital following a two-car crash on Highway 97."

As soon as the salesmen returned to their offices Pawel reviewed his listings and appointments and then studied a survey his secretary had conducted. The survey showed that majority of the taxpayer's in Penticton felt Pawel should precede building the Lakeshore Mancan Inn. While Pawel was reviewing the data, the telephone rang. He picked up the receiver after the third ring and said, "Hello."

On the other end was Mayor Edwards who began by saying; "I thought you would like to see democracy in action. City Council will vote on the third reading to rezone the property on Thursday."

Pawel was overjoyed. Not only had he convinced Peter White to be a co-venturer but the final hurdle of rezoning could be cleared within the next twenty-four hours.

"Mind you several of the aldermen are sympathetic to your wife's and Ed Ami's cause and they may have a large crowd of protesters on hand when the final reading takes place next Thursday," the Mayor continued.

It was a chilly November afternoon when several hundred protesters gathered at the Plaza Mall parking lot and began parading towards Okanagan Lake. The route took the demonstrators along Main Street, past City Hall ending on vacant land where the Lakeshore Mancan Inn was to be built. Students joined environmentalists, each carrying symbols. The demonstrators were all ages and included Sobo Birch who earlier, Principal Ami had said wasn't rehabitable. Leading the parade was a RCMP patrol car with flashing lights. Not far behind was a piper playing Scottish tunes. The piper was followed by Gloria and Ami carrying a huge sign painted in bold red and white with a sketch of the proposed hotel and the words underneath, *Protect the Environment – No Hotel Wanted.*

When the parade reached its destination police parked themselves strategically while Ami and Gloria placed a replica of the hotel on the grass and began smashing it with an axe.

"Hey, you! What do you think you're doing?" shouted a policeman waving his arms.

Other policemen soon converged to the site where the smashing was taking place. Ami and Gloria were arrested and pieces of the replica confiscated. Seeing a disturbance, TV reporters converged on the scene. As the paddy wagon arrived Ami and Gloria were being interviewed.

"We want the beech preserved," Gloria lamented. "I have never demonstrated before but it had to be done to get Penticton's attention."

"I'm not frightened and will demonstrate again if City Council approves the construction to proceed." Ami continued. When a reporter more intrepid than the others asked Ami what he thought if Council did give approval to the rezone.

"Look, if you love the outdoors, birds, parks and beaches and Ogopogo, and want to preserve them, City Council has to listen otherwise they will make an exit during the next election."

Before the paddy wagon door was closed Gloria said, "Rest assured that if City Council doesn't stop the Lakeshore Mancan Inn being built, Ami and I will demonstrate again.

It may be just as rewarding as hitch-hiking in Turkey but we'll do everything in our power to prevent Pawel interfering with Penticton's future."

As the paddy wagon was leaving Pawel shouted, "Ed and Gloria, your hearts might be in the right place but your brains are on vacation."

Gloria, after hearing the comment, shouted back, "And you Pawel, must have had an ozone layer pass over your head."

Then Pawel shot back, "If both of you are so concerned about the environment, why don't you campaign to save the whales and against acid rain, pollution of lakes and cutting of trees in forests?"


Monday morning Ami had at least three issues to deal with. First was that he noticed Joe and Moe did not respond to his affection. Second, the boys weren't doing well in classes, and third, he would have to tell the students about the weekend demonstration. During the morning ritual of welcoming students and staff, giving sports scores and highlighting student achievements over the weekend, Ami congratulated the students and said that although he and Gloria were arrested they were released an hour later.

Ami's first appointment was with a parent who said he intended to sue the basketball coach, Albert Short. The father made the announcement after the School Board agreed to formulate a policy outlining how searches would be conducted in the future.

"The School Board brushed it off in my opinion. Its attitude is, so what? I believe the coach should have been disciplined in some other way," the parent continued.

While Ami sat at his desk listening the disgruntled father continued, "The Board's other recommendation to *acknowledge* the coach's decision to search the students upsets me. To acknowledge the incident is an insane recommendation. I don't understand why one has to have a policy for something as basic as human dignity."

Ami apologized and again said; "I guess if you decide to sue, I'll see you in court. There's no use discussing the incident any further. Have a good day Mr. Wilson."

After Wilson left, Ami received an update from the music teacher, Frank Tarafski, on the chocolate sales, "During the demonstration students sold over 500 chocolate boxes. It now gives us enough money to pay for the bus. It's ours, the blue and white bus is ours."

"Congratulations, Frank," Ami said, obviously pleased.

"Without the demonstration and parade the kids wouldn't have done it. Now they will be able to go on a band tour."

"Any feedback from the kids who did the knocking?

"Well some people said they had allergies or that chocolates were fattening otherwise the sales were as usual."

As soon as Ami was through speaking with the music teacher there were two mothers waiting to see him. Both parents had deep religious convictions and the first said, "Mr. Ami, take a look at these calendars. One could almost say they were porno. The girls are from your high school."

Ami took one of the calendars and flipped through the twelve months. "Yes, these are Penticton High students. I recognize all of them."

At issue were the popular pin-up calendars, the brainchild of two home economics students, featuring a model for each month of the calendar year stressing the wholesome look.

"Okay, leave it with me. I'll look into it," Ami said to the parents as they made their exit.

And when he met with the two students they said the project was an innovative attempt at making money so teachers and students would take bus-driving lessons. "Just because there's unemployment and our economy isn't improving, doesn't mean people are going to stop living. They need some form of entertainment."

One of the girls dug into her wallet and presented Ami with a $2000 cheque.

"Here," she said, "This should cover the cost of the driving lessons."

But the day wasn't over for Ami after the two girls left, Monica handed him two letters that had not been read yet. The first dealt with students praying together at the start of the day.

A parent of one of the students wrote that as an atheist she didn't see the necessity of prayer opening at public school. In part the letter read:

To Whom It May Concern'

I don't impose my views on other people so why should I have prayer rammed down my child's throat? I wonder how many people go to church on Sunday and carry out their religious views?

The second letter Ami read dealt with the anti-hotel parade and demonstration and it was addressed to himself.

Dear Ed Ami,

Principal, Penticton High School.

As a principal you are imposing your views on the students. Students must realize that they can make a personal choice if they want the Lakeshore Mancan Inn to be built or not. You must realize also most of the students haven't got the right to vote. The School Board suggests you restrict yourself to your principalship and not leading public demonstrations.

Chairman of the Board of School Trustees

Penticton District number 15

A month later Ami appeared as a witness to a break-in at the school causing damage to the window and the lockers. The School Board had laid charges against Sobo Birch at the Small Claims Court and wanted compensation. It was 9:30 a. m. when the judge entered the Courtroom amid an atmosphere of confusion.

Those present took a cue from the Court clerk, hastily standing up to show respect, and just as quickly sit down to become part of the confusion.

The judge ran through a docket of claims asking those present to identify themselves. Most of the defendants, present and absent were individuals. Most of the plaintiffs were companies. The dress of those present ranged from jeans to business suits and everyone appeared nervous.

After the judge finished in informal roll call he dealt with the difficult cases which the defendants were absent.

And then among the cases the judge dealt with were a department store seeking settlement of delinquent accounts, a sporting goods dealer whose costumer bought uniforms for his hockey team and never paid for them and apartment landlord whose tenant paid his rent by cheque but it was NSF.

Once the default cases were completed the judge dealt with those that were contested for which the defendants came to Court. In the first, an obese woman with a Persian cat in her arms reached a stage of a shouting match with a manager of a transmission company. She claimed that a week after the transmission was installed it wrecked her car and she felt the franchisee should pay for the damage.

Following a brief intermission the case was finally settled and those in the public gallery had a difficult time keeping a straight face. To some, especially street people, the Small Claims Court was a spectator sport. Heads turned left and right, defendant then plaintiff, as each case progressed. The judge's ruling drew approval and frowns. Courtrooms often attract derelicts looking for a place to rest and Penticton was no exception. With a bottle of wine wrapped in a brown paper bag, a vagrant fell asleep and began snoring. For a moment at least all eyes in the Courtroom turned towards him until the clerk politely asked the vagrant to leave.

The following case involved two men energetically conversing in American Sign Language.
The plaintiff was deaf and the interpreter unfolded the story, as there was a misunderstanding and misinformation on both sides. The plaintiff made a rental deposit on a house but cancelled the cheque after failing to find employment.

The final case dealt with Sobo Birch who lived as a foster child at the Kent home and broke a window and damaged the lockers at Penticton High School, Sobo pleaded guilty. In passing sentence the judge said, "Fifty hours of community service. The Court stands recessed until next Monday morning." As Ami walked out of the courtroom he thought, "What a wasted day?"
And when he returned to his school the assumption was the correct one. Not only was it a wasted day but there was a picket line waiting to greet him as the teachers in Penticton and throughout District 15, had

gone on strike for higher wages. Ami believed nothing else could go wrong but it did. In addition to the strike Monica said to him. "A permit has been issued to Pawel Kowalchuk to proceed with construction of the Lakeshore Mancan Inn."

# CHAPTER TWENTY-ONE

As soon as the teachers' strike was over in 1957 Ami spent less time managing the daily affairs of the school and many of the routine chores he handed to Vice-principal Smith. Having more spare time each evening after work, one evening, Ami took Gloria to the site where the Lakeshore Mancan Inn was built and then to a nearby bingo hall where they discussed the project further. By now contractors were pouring the concrete foundation. This particular evening the hall was filled to capacity and as the first game was called Ami craned his neck noticing all sorts of participants, including Roman and Evdokia who had lucky charms with them, hoping to make a quick dollar. From where Gloria and Ami sat they had an excellent view of an electronic screen on a wall with bingo letters posted as soon as they were called. The caller wearing a white cowboy hat sat on a stage that had a table and a clear-colored glass container with numbered jumping ping-pong balls on it.

The caller had a microphone with him and as soon as "Bingo!" was hollered an attendant, who wore a baseball cap with the letters KC on it, rushed to Roman's table, called the numbers back to the caller who eventually confirmed Roman had won one-hundred dollars.

While the game was in progress Gloria and Ami glanced towards a frail-looking contestant sitting next to them. All the contestant needed was a B-12 to be a winner when three other contestants simultaneously hollered, "Bingo!"

An attendant again checked the card verifying there were three winners. When this was done, each contestant experienced a moment of exultation.

The fragile woman sitting next to Ami, however, said, "Oh, dear, all I needed was just one more number."

"Frustrating, isn't it?" Ami said.

The fragile looking woman nodded her head and with a returned curious glance asked Ami, "Don't I know you from somewhere?"

"Perhaps you do. My name is Ed Ami, principal of Penticton High. And you?"

"Of course. My foster son use to talk about you frequently. I'm Sheila Kent."

Ami expected a compliment but that was not the case when Mrs. Kent said, "I'm the one who spoke to you right after the Sadie Hawkins dance and I followed the conversation with a letter."
I forgot, who's your foster child?"
"Sobo Birch."
"Oh, him, well…"
"Well, I might as well be candid with you Mr. Ami, when Sobo fell through the ceiling in the science room you handled the case miserably. Since then I have instructed my lawyer to sue for damage."
Ami's face turned pale and used the standard answer to similar circumstances, "If that is the case I'll get to see you in Court."
"Please have your cards ready for the Bonanza game!" the caller intoned. "Extra cards may be purchased from an attendant nearest to you. In this game the entire card must be blocked out. The prize is one-thousand dollars."


Ami and Gloria each purchased extra cards and while waiting for the game to begin Ami strolled to the food bar to buy two cups of coffee. While Ami was absent a contestant sitting near Gloria said pointing to Ami, "You're not his wife? Are you?"

"No, we however, are living together."

"You are Pawel Kowalchuk's wife and work in the OR?"

"I work in the operating room but I'm not Pawel's wife any longer. We have a legal separation."

"At any rate, you work in the operating room in the Penticton General Hospital. Is that correct?"

"I do."

"And you were present when my husband was operated on?"

Gloria shrugged her shoulders. "Who is your husband?"

"The patient with the sponge left inside him, remember?"

"OR nurses as a rule don't bring their work home. It's the surgeon who operated and I assisted as a scrub nurse."

"You assisted, did you?"

"I don't understand what you're driving at."

"To put it bluntly my husband died on the operating room table and it seems someone forgot to remove the sponge before the incision was closed."

"Oh, him."

"Yes, him, and do you want to know something else?"

"What?"

"I have undertaken to sue the hospital, Dr. Alverez and you, for malpractice."

This time Gloria became pale and jittery. She had difficulty speaking so when Ami returned with the coffee she said to him, "That's it, Ed. Let's get out of here."

And they did through the back door where the camper truck was parked nearby. As Ami and Gloria walked towards the pickup camper Gloria remained silent and seemed worried. Noticing Gloria's behavior Ami took her by the arm and said, "Gloria, let's go for a drive."

"An excellent idea," Gloria answered and the two chose a route, which circled Skaha Lake on the outskirts of Penticton.

As soon as they reached a viewpoint on Highway 97 Ami asked, "Shall we stop here?"

Gloria agreed. Once parked they had a panoramic view of Skaha Lake and the Penticton Airport which was lit up in blue waiting for a Boeing 737 to land while on a flight from Vancouver to Calgary.

Both Ami and Gloria had been burned with lawsuits so they stayed at the viewpoint until the bitter December winds began to drift through the Okanagan Valley and then Gloria said, "I'm hungry. Let's drive to Okanagan Falls where it may be a bit warmer."

As soon as Ami started the pickup camper, and left the scenic viewpoint overlooking Skaha Lake, Highway 97 turned eastward around a mountain and came to a steep hill, and then the village of Okanagan Falls itself. Although there were no falls in the community fruit trees lined the streets and avenues and there was the popular Okanagan Falls Restaurant where Ami and Gloria stopped and seemed to enjoy themselves. It was past 10:00 p.m. when each ordered a roast beef sandwich.

"To go with the roast beef, have you any wine?" Ami asked the waiter.

"We do but only six bottles left, that's all."

"We'll have a bottle."

The waiter opened a compartment and lifted out a bottle. While pointing at the bottle the waiter said, "Very old and revered."

After Ami studied the shape of the bottle he excitedly said, "Good heavens. That's Pride of The Okanagan – Vintage 1919. It's a wine my father vinted to commemorate the end of World War 1."

"How much does a bottle cost?" Gloria asked.

"It's not cheap any more, $100." Ami handed the waiter two fifty-dollar bills and then the waiter brought two crystal glasses and placed them in front of Ami and Gloria. The wine was already chilled so the waiter took out the corkscrew and poured some into each glass. As soon as Gloria had a sip she smacked her lips and said, "Very, very good."

The thought of going through a teachers' strike, the Lakeshore Inn being built and the two of them being sued, drove Ami and Gloria to drink more than usual.

Near midnight Ami and Gloria got into the pickup camper and headed home towards Penticton via the east side of Skaha Lake, while on the right, there were homes next to cliffs and sandbanks and higher still, all sorts of trees: pine hemlock and cedar grew tall.

As they drove along Gloria said, "That's Penticton in the distance. Isn't it beautiful at night all lit up? And it's so quiet, as we drive along; there even isn't the sound of an owl and crickets chirping."

As they drove onward something more inner than crickets chirping or the scene before them came to their attention when Ami exclaimed, "Look! I think I'm seeing a ghost."

Gloria took her head from Ami's shoulder. "Ed, I think you are right it is a ghost." They each took a deep breath and seconds later Gloria screamed, "Look it's coming directly at us."

Ami and Gloria were passing a cemetery at the time and were astonished to have headlights of the camper reflected back into their eyes.

Almost blinded, Ami was able to steer the vehicle to a curb, stop, and turn off the lights. Seconds later he said, "Look, it has disappeared."

After several minutes of waiting Ami decided it was safe to move on but when he turned on the engine the reflection was back and much brighter this time. Frightened, Ami turned off the lights and Gloria edged in closer to his side where she said, "My father said aspirations are often associated with individuals who had suffered an unusual demise."

"Whatever it is, it certainly not a guardian angel. I have never seen a ghost like this one before."

"You are right. It's something strange. Sit still," Gloria continued.

In the present mood and state of mind, even if the sky had fallen it would not have troubled Ami and Gloria more. Both were still frightened and if they could would have escaped the world to live on another planet. But ten minutes had passed and the headlights were turned on again. This time the reflection did not appear so Ami began driving again. While driving he said, "We better keep this to ourselves or else people will think we are crazy."

Gloria thought the figure that appeared before them was a premonition of an impending disaster.

"I hope something doesn't happen to us by the time we reach home," she said.

Ami's response was, "I wouldn't worry," as Gloria continued, "Patients have told me about ghosts while in the operating room. I just laughed at the time and said to them it was probably Dr. Singh running in his underwear. Some thought they saw oil on the road or static electricity. Others believed it was a signal and a bad sign to see a ghost while traveling."

"Whatever it was that we saw it sure frightened us," Ami said as he pressed on the accelerator. As they drove further Gloria continued, "The wine, Pride of the Okanagan – vintage 1919 has made me sleepy."

Ami yawned and said that he too had difficulty staying awake and applied more pressure to the accelerator as he was approaching a crest of a steep hill.

The speedometer read 60 miles an hour and when it reached 70 the pickup camper began to swerve. It crossed the centre line at 80 as a school bus was coming towards it. All of a sudden glaring headlights turned into a crash. A crash in which the bus driver, Frank Tarafski, was seriously injured but not Gloria or Ami who suffered only a severe bruise to his sore right knee.

That night while in a bed in an upstairs bedroom Ami said to Gloria, "We should have taken a taxi home as soon as we realized we had too much Pride of the Okanagan – Vintage 1919 wine to enjoy and began seeing a ghost".

"A ghost followed by the school bus crash. The shock still creeps on to me too," Gloria said as she pulled the light switch and it became dark.

Ami and Gloria kept tossing and turning and then the wind began to whistle outside. It was 2:00 a. m. when Gloria said, "Listen, I hear footsteps."

She regretted the door was left unlocked and a chill quickly ran up and down her spine.

At first believing it was the ghost they encountered by Skaha Lake and then changed her mind, thinking it were Joe and Moe who were sleeping in an adjacent room.

"Joe or Moe, is that you?" she called out but no one answered the call.

'It's just the house creaking and the wind outside," Ami assured his covivant allaying any fears Gloria may have had.

Just as they were drifting into slumber Gloria was startled another time as she heard the footsteps again.

"Hush," she said and both listened. A strange thing was happening. Unmistakably something was either climbing or going downstairs.

"I can't take this any longer," Ami said and turned on the lights. There was nothing there. The footstep sound had stopped. As Ami got out of bed he stumbled and fell. When he picked himself up he stuck his head through the door and hollered, "Are you the ghost we saw on the road near Okanagan Falls, or is it you, Joe and Moe?"

Gloria afraid to be alone whispered, "Don't leave me Ed." But he paid no attention and ran down a flight of stairs. Shivering in her nightgown Gloria followed him to the kitchen where they found a note on the table that read,

"Sorry Mom. We hate this place and have gone to live with Dad."

As soon as Ami and Gloria crawled back into bed Ami said, "Well, how about Joe and Moe?"

"I wouldn't worry. I'll get them back as soon as I speak to my lawyer," Gloria said.

The following week, in Family Court Pawel said to Judge Klinkhammer that Joe and Moe had packed their clothing and moved in with him into the apartment on Scott Street. "It wasn't a kidnapping, your Honor. Not only were the boys afraid of ghosts who frequent Ami's house but also their mother is explosive and temperamental."

"Who has custody of the boys at the moment?" Judge Klinkhammer, a tall, slender man, partially bald, and wearing steel-rimmed spectacles, asked both parents.

'The mother," Pawel replied and as he was speaking recalled a salesmen tour of the home the judge occupied and a Doberman pinscher tied up in the furnace room which at the time drew his ire. Many times Pawel wondered if a judge could be so cruel to an animal, how could he, as a judge, be kind to people. When Pawel finished giving his side of Joe and Moe's return to his care, the judge then turned towards Gloria and said, "Mrs. Kowalchuk, let's hear your side of the story concerning your sons."

Gloria was articulate and spoke for several minutes. Her final words were, "The case today, your Honor, had nothing to do with me living with Ed Ami but with Pawel abducting Joe and Moe who I love dearly."
Judge Klinkhammer seemed impressed with what Gloria had said. Turning to Pawel he then asked, "Since your separation are you living with someone else?"
"No, your Honor."
And as a real estate salesman who is involved in the Lakeshore Mancan Inn project, you are out of town a lot."
"Yes, sir."
After several minutes of questions and answers pertinent to the case, Judge Klinkhammer faced Pawel and said, "Since your former wife has custody of the boys already. The Court has no alternative but

order you to return Joe and Moe to live with their mother.

"I understand too that you aren't home much of the time therefore the Court orders that you return Joe and Moe to their mother within the next twenty-four hours."

Gloria's face reflected joy while Pawel's sadness. He was disappointed with the Court's decision and as he was leaving the Courtroom said to himself, "The judge acts as a policeman, prosecutor, and witness and has power to lock up an offender for life. Although his ruling can be appealed one would take up a lot of my time. I have a deadline to meet, as I want to have the Lakeshore Mancan Inn completed by October when the Canadian Real Estate Association will hold a meeting in Penticton."

"Well, Gloria. How did it go?" Ami asked.

"Terrific. Dr. Alverez was cleared on a charge of malpractice and as his scrub nurse, I was also cleared. And how about your case with Mrs. Kent?"

Ami was ecstatic too. Sobo Birch who had fallen through the ceiling in the science room, according to Judge Klinkhammer climbed there at his own risk knowing he had no business taking Shirley Philips there."

"Fabulous!" Gloria exclaimed. "Now that we have been cleared of any wrong let's go to sleep."

Ami turned off the *Eleven O'clock* TV News. The anchorman had already accurately described what had happened at the Ami and Gloria's separate trials. Ami gave Gloria an anxious looked and crawled into bed. A feeling of devastation and an eeriness feeling crept over him as minutes later he thought Joe and Moe were eavesdropping.

"It's just impossible to be alone any longer," he said.

"Isn't it the truth?" Gloria agreed, put on her housecoat and then knocked on Joe and Moe's door but there was no response.

Ami knocked the second time, "Joe and Moe, "I want to speak to you."

Joe finally answered, "About what?"

"Privacy."

"Oh, privacy?" Moe groaned, unlocked and poked his head through the door.

"Yes, privacy. And if I catch one of you sneaking up to our room I'll….

"You'll what?"

"I'll be forced to take severe measures."

"Why wait until next time?" Joe joined in the conversation, opened the door wider and punched Ami a hard blow to Ami's face. Ami missed Joe's second blow but not the one from Moe and the three rolled down a flight of stairs where further blows were exchanged. "That's what you get for breaking Mom's and Dad's marriage!" Joe retorted.

Gloria who was standing at the bottom of the stirs said, "I'll call police," wishing now that she didn't have Joe and Moe's custody.

When two constables arrived, the first asked Joe, Where's your father?"

Gloria quickly answered, "He's in Winnipeg." Pointing to Joe and Moe she continued, "Please take them away."

The constable was hesitant. This is a domestic dispute. Police as a rule don't like to get involved in family arguments."

Glancing at Ami who besides having a broken nose, red cheeks and blood on his housecoat, the second cop said, "Mr. Ami, are you all right?"

Ami moaned, "I'm okay. I can handle them. Thanks for coming just the same."

When the second policeman saw Ami's pajamas ripped to shreds he gasped and said," "You may lay charges against the boys if you wish."

"Do that," Gloria said.

As soon as Ami approved Joe and Moe were handcuffed and taken to the police station where they were interrogated and charged with causing bodily harm. They would spend the night at the Child Centre until a court was held. From a grieving mother Gloria had turned into a viper.

Two days later the Joe and Moe case was the first on the docket and Ami and Gloria arrived just in time for Judge Klinkhammer to ask, "Who is pressing charges against the boys?"

"I am," Ami replied.

The judge looked down at the boys, "You have been in this court room before?"

"We have," Joe replied.

"And what have you got to say for yourselves this time, Joe first."

Joe gave their side of the story what had happened, which wasn't complementary to their mother or Ami.

"After spending ten minutes on questions and answers pertinent to the charge Judge Klinkhammer banged his gavel and said, "After listening to both sides and all facts, the Court has no alternative but to impose a sentence of fifty hours of community service and for each to read a book of their choice within a month. Beginning tomorrow you will clean the stables at the Scarborough Riding Stables. There is nothing else to say."

"But there is, your Honor," Moe said.

Curious, the judge said, "What?"

"Shoveling manure at Scarborough Stables isn't community work. The stable is privately owned by a probation officer whose name is Justin Watson."

The boys agreed they were guilty of harming Ami but argued that their sentence should have a community project in mind and not profit an individual."

"Helping the elderly, cutting grass in the park or manning the Crises line," Moe suggested.

Judge Klinkhammer, a stubborn man, put his spectacles on, and looked down at the boys again and said, "Because of your attitude I double your sentence to one-hundred hours. Next case please."

As Joe and Moe were leaving the courtroom they regretted their father wasn't present to defend them.

After Joe and Moe spent a Saturday at the Scarborough Stables and were relaxing in their bedroom, Gloria and Ami were angered by the loudness of their stereo.

As they were listening to the music in the distance a headline in the Penticton *Herald* caught their attention: *Rock Music Obsession Haunted Teen's Last Days*.

The article dealt with a Penticton High School youth who liked Kwitka's music so much that he wrote a note that her music is played at his funeral following a suicide.

The note in part read: "Please don't blame my friends. I shall be buried with my Kwitka album."

According to the article the teenager placed a 12-guage shotgun under his chin and shot himself.

The boy told his friends before killing himself that he was looking forward meeting Kwitka at the official opening at the Lakeshore Mancan Inn but it was too long of a time period to wait.

The boy's death was especially puzzling to Gloria which led her to say, "Ami, I wonder what type of music Joe and Moe are into these days?"

Gloria realized that there was friction in her relationship with her sons and that they too enjoyed Kwitka's music.

According to Ami the teenager who committed suicide was a normal boy who was a member of the basketball team and was part of the High School band.

"Personally I can't stand listening to Kwitka's rock n roll records. The subliminal satanic messages in them are what did it," Ami then said.

"You might be right," Gloria agreed. "We better check out what Joe and Moe are playing."

And both rushed up a flight of stairs and entered Joe and Moe's room without knocking. They found Joe and Moe each reading a copy of *All the Murders in The Bible* by an unknown author. They were complying with what Judge Klinkhammer ordered them to do. Hearing the loud music in the background and then seeing the title of the book, Gloria became ballistic and screamed, "Its Kwitka's music that's doing it!"

"Doing what?" Moe asked.

"Causing suicides."

Joe and Moe kept on reading and studying pictures of Cain killing his brother, Abel; Isaac discovering Esau's murder of his brother, Jacob; the slaying of Isera, Saul killing himself, how Absolom was killed, Jehu slaying Joram and Jezebel tossed out a window.

Gloria rushed towards the stereo, picked up an album and after reading the title said, "Just as I thought, it's Kwitka's latest album.

She took the album of the turntable and smashed it against the hardwood floor.

"There's nothing but evil spirits in Kwitka's music," she said

Joe responded with, "Oh, Mom, I hate your heart.  I bought this album with my last dollar, after all Kwitka is our aunt."

Moe joined in, "We have nothing against the world but are tired of shoveling manure for Mr. Watson. When I think of it, ever since you and Ed consumed that bottle of Pride of

Okanagan wine both of you have gone, what shall I say, strange?"

Joe echoed those sentiments. "And we are tired of being picked on since the two of you started to go out together."

Gloria gave Joe a whack across the face for the comment he made. "Take that!" she said and continued, "Both of you, get out, leave! I'm fed up with the way the two of you behave! That's it"

"But we are reading a book like Judge Klinkhammer ordered us to do," Joe said.

"The judge meant reading Shakespeare, Jane Austin or Charles Dickens and not literature you are presently reading."

Gloria picked up the books and tossed them out the window and then gestured with her hands, "If you'd be happier living with your father, go ahead. I repeat, out, out, out. I don't want you in my and Ami's house any longer."

It was 9:13 p.m. when Joe and Moe accepted the challenged and simultaneously replied, "Okay, Mom, we'll move out of here"

But they had nowhere to go.

Joe and Moe put on their jean jackets and slowly walked towards the downtown core of Penticton.

Pawel thought he was a winner on all fronts. Sitting in Paul White's office in Winnipeg, he was delighted what he had achieved. White had placed into a bank the balance of funds necessary to build the Lakeshore Mancan Inn in Penticton.

With City Council approval given, the foundation already poured and the outer structure completed, Pawel was anxiously waiting for the day when the Inn would be officially opened.
He was sitting at a desk with Mr. White believing nothing in his world would go wrong but it did when the telephone rang. White picked up he receiver and after saying, "Hello," handed the receiver to Pawel and a long-distance operator at the other end said, "Mr. Kowalchuk please. Long distance is calling from Penticton, British Columbia." "I'm him," Pawel replied thinking it was a client who enquired about leasing space on the first floor once the Lakeshore Mancan Inn

was completed. He was disappointed, however, when the voice on the line said, "This is Sergeant Kevin Brown speaking.  Is this Pawel Kowalchuk?"

"Speaking."

"You have sons by the name of Joseph and Maurice?"

"I do, what about them?"

"They have been charged with breaking, entering and possession of drugs."

"I can't believe it.  Are you certain you have charged the right teenagers?"

For a moment Pawel could not speak as pictures of cocaine, heroin and amphetamines raced through his mind. "Are Joe and Moe all right?"

'They're at the Penticton Child Centre and have confessed to the crimes."

"Police have a written statement from them?"

"They do."

And their rights were explained:"

"They were."

"Does their mother know about the incident?"

"She does and I believe she may be the cause of their predicament."

"How did you reach that conclusion?"

"Well, last night she apparently kicked Joe and Moe out of Ed Ami's home. Having nowhere to go they strolled into the Acme Record Store where they met two male undesirables.'

"And then what had happened?"

"The strange men offered them a place to stay, food and drugs."

"That's dreadful."

"And there's more," the sergeant said. "These men wanted rent and food money so they had Joe and Moe steal a television set and sold it to a pawn shop."

Pawel was upset the way his family was disintegrating. "May I ask another question?"

"Go ahead."

"The home which the boys were taken too, is it on Norton Street?"

"It was."

"And from which home did they steal the television?"

"Tina Kent is her name, a widow on Government Street. It's the home which until recently was the residence for that rangy-tang kid, I forget his name."

"Sobo Birch?"

"That's the one."

Then the sergeant said that Moe and Joe were scheduled to appear in Family Court the following day and that it would be worthwhile for Pawel to contact the probation officer, Justin Watson.

"I'll do that," Pawel said. "Better still I'll take the first flight available to Penticton and speak to him in person."

The time was 9:10 p. m. Pawel had forty-five minutes in which to leave the Mancan office, catch a taxi to the Winnipeg Airport and board a plane. It was 3:30 a. m. by the time Pawel arrived in Penticton. He slept until eight and then headed for the Child Centre where Joe and Moe spent the night.


"Please come in," the Supervisor at the Child Centre said as soon as Pawel entered the reception area. "I'm Gordon Kennedy." Following formal introductions Pawel asked if he could speak to Joe and Moe.

"I'm sorry as the social worker, Fran List, is interviewing the boys. As soon as she's through, of course you may speak to them." While Pawel was waiting he picked up a public telephone and arranged an appointment with probation officer, Justin Watson for 1:00 p. m. The boys were scheduled to appear in court at 1.30.

As soon as Mrs. List was through doing her interview she opened the door to the conference room and seeing Pawel said, "Please come inside, Mr. Kowalchuk, I'm delighted to meet the boys' father. My name is Fran List."

"How do you do?" Pawel said while shaking her hand.

"Now the matter on hand, Mr. Kowalchuk, "You understand the seriousness of the offenses committed by your sons," Mrs. List said.

"Pawel said he wasn't certain so Mrs. List continued, "Joe and Moe's behavior is not socially acceptable and I'm going to suggest to the probation officer, Justin Watson, who will in turn make a recommendation to Judge Klinkhammer, that Joe and Moe be made a ward of the government until further notice and placed into a group home."

"Really, their behavior, whose fault is it, mother or father?"

"Both."

"How did you reach that conclusion?"
"Because are both hard working parents. Mrs. Kowalchuk is extremely busy at the hospital and protesting to halt construction of the Lakeshore Mancan Inn. And you are promoting it, but are out of town a great deal. If the boys were shown more affection by their parents it is unlikely they would have to appear before Judge Klinkhammer so often."
What could Pawel say? There was some truth in the comment. Finally Mrs. List said, ``I'll see you and the boys at the courthouse at one-thirty."


Once alone Pawel, Joe and Moe discussed what had happened the night before, the upcoming court appearance and if the arresting policeman advised them of their rights to seek a lawyer.
"No lawyer spoke to us," Joe said.
"And we admitted to breaking, entering, stealing and smoking marijuana. But we were forced to do it," Joe continued.
"Forced? By whom?"
"Crash London and Boomer Grissom."
"And why were you forced?"
"To cover the rent and cost of the food."

Pawel met the probation office on time. Justin Watson's office was situated on the second floor of the Court House and not a far distance from where the Lakeshore Mancan Inn was now almost 50% completed.

"I'm glad you could make it Mr. Kowalchuk. Watson began as he pulled out a file from his desk with the words 'Joe and Moe Kowalchuk' on it. "I'll be candid with you. I'm going recommend to Judge Klinkhmmer that your sons be put into a group home for a period of six months."

"That long?"

"Well, their file is getting thicker each time. Unless you can suggest an alternative?"

Pawel said he could. "Have Gloria release their custody and I promise you sir, that I'll enroll the boys into a private boarding school. And may I suggest that Joe and Moe do more community work but make certain the work doesn't profit an individual like yourself."

"Did I hear you correctly?  You did say you would enroll them at a private school?"

"One that is operated by the Silesian order of priests. This way their schooling wouldn't be interrupted"

Watson dressed in blue jeans, a buttoned up white shirt, and cowboy boots with a speck of manure on them, thought for a moment and then replied, "I have a problem with your proposal. You see, Mr. Kowalchuk, I'd like to give your sons a break but they faced Judge Klinkhammer twice before and Gloria still has legal custody."

Pawel understood the problem and hoped the judge would too.

Five minutes later Mrs. List appeared in the courtroom along with Gloria. Pawel was disappointed that legal counsel didn't represent the boys so he would have to act as their agent

On cue from the courtroom clerk everyone quickly stood up and when the clerk said, "British Columbia Court, Family Division, Judge Klinkhammer presiding," those present sat down as quickly as they stood up.

Watson, Mrs. List, Gloria and Pawel sat at a rectangular table facing the judge. Joe and Moe sat at a separate table but also faced the judge.

After Pawel was through pleading Joe and Moe's case Judge Klinkhammer turned towards Gloria and asked, "Is there anything else that you would like to say, Mrs. Kowalchuk?"

Gloria shook her head. Her theory was less said the better. Having no objections from Gloria the judge asked Mrs. List and Justin Watson if they had any last words. Both replied that Joe and Moe should be sent to a group home for six months. The home had a rehab program and supervised group parents Rosie and Dan Pearson.

Those at the home were expected to do chores, split wood, get rid of elm trees with Dutch elm disease, demolish an old building and do a lot of jogging.

As soon as the court adjourned Pawel met the probation officer in the hallway and said to him. "Mr. Watson, now that Judge Klinkhammer has sentenced Joe and Moe six months to a group home I want you to place yourself in their situation."

"What do you mean?"

"They are sixteen years of age and penned up with adult offenders. To tell you the truth I'm concerned about Joe and Moe's safety and welfare."

"Why is that?"

"I was told by those who have spent time at this particular Group Home that the group father is kind of…"

Watson interrupted, "Kind of what?"

"Kind of a fruit cake, if you know what I mean."

"Hog wash. Mr. Pearson is an excellent caretaker with ten years' experience."

After more discussion about the Group Home Watson said, "As a probation officer I want you, Mr. Kowalchuk, not to contemplate kidnapping the boys or interfere with justice. Any intensions that way may find you in contempt of a court decision."

"That's if you can define the word *contempt* for me. As far as Judge Klinhammer's decision calling my boys derogatory names during the sentencing I object to that. It seems to me the judge speaks like a virtual monarch over the court he reigns and I believe his ex-cathedra remarks exceed his duty."

Watson was surprised the way Pawel felt. "Why should you feel that way?"

Pawel's reply was, "Why shouldn't a judge face public scrutiny? This court was at a public expense. Are you telling me, Mr.

Watson, I can't criticize a judge? What nonsense."

# CHAPTER TWENTY-TWO

Ami phoned and said, "Gloria, I'll be home late."

When Gloria asked why he replied. "Frank Tarafsky and I are discussing an important plan to purchase another school bus."

Joe and Moe were no longer living with their mother and Ami and that was okay.

Everything seemed quiet; including the stereo until an eighty-mile an hour turbulent wind swept the Okanagan Valley and silenced every bird, animal and insect. Because of the force of the wind shutters slammed, eaves and rafters creaked and groaned. Winds weren't unusual in Penticton but with such velocity it also scattered garbage cans, garden utensils and wine barrels and bottles and split cedar shingles and damaging the stucco siding of the buildings.

Although it was still an hour before supper, every fruit tree, vine, hedge and bush seemed to worship the ground as the wind was accompanied by roaring and rumbling thunder, lighting and rain. The storm nearly rocked Ami's home from its foundation, and eve troughs couldn't handle the water.

Watching the storm through the living room window, Gloria said to herself, "Ed will have a difficult time coming home in the storm. It's a primeval downpour, a storm of deluge proportions, similar to the one Noah experienced in the *Bible*."

It seemed thunderbolts and flashes of lightning were everywhere. The scene was like in the dream Pharaoh had when seven scrawny cows ate seven fat cows and seven undersized ears of corn swallowed seven hardy full ears.

At the peak of the storm Ami completed his meeting with Tarafasky and was heading home from the High School. Because of the storm he was involved in a three-car pileup at the intersection of Main and Lakeshore Drive. The street was slippery and wet. As a result of the crash Ami was taken to Emergency at the Penticton Regional Hospital by ambulance. When he arrived Dr. Singh was already waiting. Besides minor scratches, bruises and a headache Ami complained about a pain to his right knee.

An X-ray was taken and while examining it Dr. Singh said, "Doesn't look good. Mr. Ami."

The condition of the knee was puzzlement to Ami and wondered why he was in Emergency at all. To him the pain was such a small thing and was perturbed Dr. Singh gave the knee so much attention.

"Let's see the knee again," Dr. Singh said. Ami rolled up a pant leg. Dr. Singh bent over for a closer look and as he probed with his finger Ami cried out, "Ouch!"

Dr. Singh looked up. "Hurts? Has the knee been injured before?""

"It does but it didn't hurt much at the time."

"When?"

"A month ago when my pickup camper and a school bus collided on the east side of Skaha Lake."

"Tell me more."

"My knee began to swell following the accident but since there was little pain I didn't do anything."

"Please continue."

"The knee began to fill with fluid and when I showed it Gloria, pressure had built to the point where she had to drain it

Once the knee was drained the pain went away and everything seemed normal until this evening when I rear-ended a car in front of me."

"Visibility was poor?"

"It certainly was."

Dr. Singh moved closer to the window and held the x-ray negative to the light. "There's an irregularity in your knee joint," he said, peered again and brought the negative for Ami to see. While they looked together Dr. Sing said, "There, that little spot confirms something is wrong with the cartilage that isn't healing properly."

Ami was suspicious. "Does that mean cancer?"

Dr. Singh shrugged his shoulder. "We'll have to consult with Dr. Alverez who specializes in things like that."

An uneasy chill of fear began to grip Ami. "If it's cancer will my leg have to be amputated?"

"If it is, amputation may be necessary but until we hear from Dr. Alverez, don't worry."

Ami's fear turned to sorrow while Dr. Singh phoned Gloria and then admitted him into a private room.

Because of the storm Gloria did not come to the hospital until after midnight. Until that time Ami laid awake wondering if the knee was cancerous. He had heard Gloria use the words *asteogeneci sarcoma* frequently. If the diagnosis of the knee was what he feared the most would it mean Ami had a malignant tumor and it might spread.

It perhaps already did to other parts of the body. In that event statistics showed Ami had another year to live. Amputation would be his only hope and even after the amputation his health would deteriorate.

While waiting for the final word from Dr. Alverez, Ami took Gloria by the hand and said, "Oh my God, I hope it's not malignant." It was early in the morning while Gloria was sitting by Ami's bedside that Dr. Singh entered the room accompanied with Dr. Alverez.

Concerned, Ami asked, "Well, what's the news?"

Dr. Alverez said that he and Dr. Singh had viewed the x-rays and an amputation would have to be performed.

"Is it benign or malignant?"

Dr. Alverez did not allay Ami's greatest fear. "Malignant."

"So when do we amputate the leg?"

"First thing tomorrow morning," Dr. Alverez replied. He had already discussed the operation with the anesthetist.

The following morning, the anesthetist in the Operating Room gave Dr. Alverez the signal to proceed with the operation that lasted one hour but to no avail.  Six months later Ed Ami died, and during his funeral Gloria said, "Ed believed he had beaten cancer but it spread to his prostrate, abdomen and brain. Through his final weeks Ed hung to hope.  The shooting pains began as soon as he was involved in a motor vehicle accident during a storm and rushed by ambulance to the Penticton General Hospital, I knew it was out of my hands.  He died at 8:45 in the morning."

# CHAPTER TWENTY-THREE

At that point Gloria's desire to stop construction of the Lakeshore Mancan Inn disappeared. From that day onward, she had only nice things to say about the Inn as the building got higher and higher. A month after Ami's funeral, relying on Pawel's experience as a realtor, Gloria asked Pawel to, "List my house and acreage for sale."

"But is it your property?" Pawel queried.

"It is, Ed willed it to me before he died."

In that case I would be delighted to market *your* property," Pawel said to Gloria over a cup of coffee and both signed a six-month listing agreement. A month after the signing, Joe and Moe found themselves in a state of shock, not because their parents were speaking to each or a rumor that their parents would reconciled their differences, but because they found Sobo Birch's body hanging at the Group home.

Sobo Birch was an acquaintance of Joe and Moe at Penticton High.

He was also a permanent ward of the government since he was taken away as a child from a single parent mother and had lived in at least a dozen foster homes and institutions since that time but he had loved the Kent home in Penticton best of all.

The Group Home parents, Rosie and Dan Pearson, were in shock too and said the teenager was receiving no psychiatric help at the time of his death although records showed he had attempted suicide previously. As soon as the body was discovered Rosie Pearson phoned Mrs. List at Human Resources complaining about the social worker.

Mrs. List had belittled her plea for help.

"I can't recall a more tragic death in all my life", Rosie said clutching a telephone tightly and scolding the social worker vociferously. "I have reservations about the way Sobo's case was handled from the onset."

The Group Home father, Dan Pearson, a heavyset man, came on the line and participated in the conversation.

"Look, Mrs. List," he said, "The entire affair with Sobo Birch placed in our group home has been bungled from start to finish."

When Mrs. List asked, "How did Sobo die?" he replied, "Sobo nailed a 2 x 4 between two dying elm trees that were about to be cut down. He suspended a rope from the top, and believe me, it was a pathetic sight."

Then Rosie complained, "When we contacted you at Human Resources the first time Sobo attempted suicide, you, Mrs. List, said it was probably only a prank."

"What is even worse," Dan Pearson took over, "When we called probation officer Justin Watson, he said he wasn't sorry for, quote, 'The little bastard'."

"And when we called the RCMP several minutes ago: Dan Pearson cut in, " Sergeant Brown said police would have to leave the boy hanging for five hours before they would take the body down to determine if there was foul play."

"Did you touch Sobo?" Mrs. List asked and was told, "The only time we touched Sobo was when he misbehaved."

Aside from the vandalism at Penticton High School Sobo Birth was practically unknown in most of Penticton but he left a notebook Moe found laying on the ground by one of the elm trees which was a damning indictment of the child welfare system.

Sobo left a tragic legacy and in the notebook described child abuse in government foster and group homes: a lack of food, overwork, beatings and miserable accommodation in homes which took the children, in some instances, as a means to supplement their own low income. Sobo Birch's notebook in part read as follows:

"I have been hurt so many times so I learned the art of blocking out all my emotions," is how the first page began. Sobo was a government ward in different communities. In the following pages his notebook spelled out graphically how the 16 year old had spent and read as follows.

"I was born in Edmonton, Alberta, that much I'm certain because of my birth certificate. I have no memories of what happened over the next several years although I know I was born of a single parent mother and later placed in my first foster home.

When I was five I remember playing with matches when the shed where I was playing caught on fire. When the fire was finally was put out I got a whipping of my life and it was made clear to me that if I ever played with matches again the beating would be worse next time.

In another home, years later, I was caught smoking. I was punished and had to smoke a package of cigarettes within half an hour. I had to inhale every drag and when I did, I was sick for a couple of days but that in itself is another story.

The next home was near Osoyoos, which was good in several ways but bad in others. I remember one night I wasn't fed and there was a box of peaches in the basement, so I ate them instead. The lady of the house got angry because she was unable to make a peach pie the following day.

In another home, I remember hauling gravel to fix the driveway and I had to tramp all the rocks and bumps with my bare feet. After I was finished I was paid fifty cents and ran as fast as I could to nearest corner store and purchase all the candy I could eat. Again I got sick.

Later, I was sent to a home in Peachland and began spending a lot of time alone. To celebrate my first anniversary with my foster parents they put on a party to mark the occasion so we each had a glass full of Prime of the Okanagan wine – vintage 1919, to enjoy. After I drink a full glass, I felt as though I was standing in the middle of a canoe during a ferocious storm on Okanagan Lake and saw a ghost. I can't remember more of that night except that it was frightening and the foster parents said it was just a dream that had.

Y next move was a year later, and I ended up living with Mr. and Mrs. Kent in Penticton. Mr. Kent was a helicopter pilot but he died in an accident, and I was told to move on.

I enjoyed Kent's home but while living here and attending High School things got a little difficult.

I was constantly in trouble with Principal Ed Ami for fighting, painting graffiti signs and breaking into lockers. Because of the damage I had done I had to go to Court and Judge Klinhammer sentenced me to do 100 hours of community work.

Soon I started missing classes and went inner tube riding on the Okanagan River channel. Near the channel there was a hillside constantly covered with marmots.

One day I was romping with my dog, Rex, and we saw one going into a hole and we began to dig and after an hour, reached its nest. As I grabbed the critter it sank its teeth into my hand and refused to let go. I beat its head with a stick and when it finally let go, Rex chewed it to ribbons for making my hand into minced meat.

And when it was Halloween party time at Pen High I met this chick named Shirley Philips so we climbed into the attic above the science room. Unfortunately while we were in the attic a tile gave way and we fell to the floor. A short time later, the social worker, Mrs. List, heard about our puppy love affair and asked me how long it would take for me to get ready and move on to a Group Home. I answered, 'several hours' but should have said 'never' because I realized the Kent home was the best I ever had.
When Mrs. List said that Shirley was pregnant and Mrs. Kent was a widow and could no longer keep me, which bothered me. I had two hours to say 'Goodbyes' to Mrs. Kent but before I did, I went to my room and dug out my harmonica and played a sad tune.

Halfway through *Amazing Grace* my lips began to quiver and shake, and then I began to cry. I even didn't stop crying when Mrs. Kent heard me.

She came to my room and tried to comfort me, but when she put her arms around me, I pulled away and told her I was going to run away. But where could I go? The Kent home was the best I ever had. I didn't want anyone, even Mrs. Kent, to love me anymore. I had been hurt so many times that all I wanted to do was to die.


I remember when Mrs. List arrived and took me to the Group Home. She wanted to talk to the Group Home parents alone, so I waited in the car. When she returned she called me to come out but I wouldn't move.

When Mrs. List came closer I refused to open the door. I didn't want to be left in the Group Home because I had heard bad things about the place.

I was alone, frightened and had no one to turn too. Mrs. List told the Group Home parents that I would get over the way I felt. Finally she coaxed me out of her car. I will never forget the way I felt at the time, no never."

The Group Home parents, Rosie and Dan Pearson, took me into the home and showed me where I would sleep. As soon as I walked into my bedroom I was horrified. The floor was covered with water about two inches deep and there were boards on the floor to keep one's feet from getting wet. The walls were painted red and peeling, and the ceiling white. The windows, which weren't larger than an atlas, had a crack. The narrow bed was a foot off the floor and instead of a blanket there was a sleeping bag on top. There was a 40-watt light bulb in the ceiling which one had to pull a string to switch the light on. The room was something one expected to see in a horror movie. There were spiders in shadowy corners and when darkness came, the cockroaches were all over. "You'll be sharing this room with two other teenaged boys, Joe and Moe Kowalchuk," the Group Home father said as soon as I lay on the bed to rest. The first night in the Group Home was a nightmare in itself. The wind constantly blew through the cracked window and the ceiling tiles were about to fall down. It was cold and spiders kept crawling onto my face. In the morning, I kept telling myself that I was experiencing a bad dream and someday soon would wake up in a home like I use to enjoy with Mr. and Mrs. Kent.

At the Group Home I felt I was living in jail. I was lonely, depressed and began to think serious about suicide, and used a razor blade to cut my arm but it hurt so much that I didn't do it again. I began missing classes at school and one day when I returned to the Group Home Mr. Pearson came into my bedroom and made a pass at me. I objected, so he slapped my face and expected me to cry. Instead I walked away as he stood there alone. It struck me that I could kill myself and no one would know what happened until it was too late.

Slowly I crept into a garage, found a rope and climbed onto the rafters. After I had secured the rope I climbed down and placed a barrel underneath. Then I climbed onto the rafters again and said a prayer asking God to take care of me. I was determined to go through with it this time so I placed a rope around my neck and kicked away from the rafter and the barrel underneath.

My lungs felt as if they were about to burst and my ears like they were melting into my head. Finally I blacked out and was engulfed in a blanket of black. I woke up sometime later and saw a lot of people standing around me. When I heard Dr. Singh say, 'How are you Sobo'? I knew I was in a hospital. Two nurses came running into my room and one of them was Mrs. Kowalchuk, the OR nurse. I recalled marching in a parade to stop construction of the Lakeshore Mancan Inn. Mrs. Kowalchuk unstrapped my body and held me in her arms telling me everything was going to turn out all and not to be afraid. I asked Mrs. Kowalchuk how I ended up in the hospital and she explained that My Group home parents, Rosie and Dan Pearson, had made an emergency phone call.

When I asked Mrs. Kowalchuk about Joe and Moe she felt repentant about being cruel to them and said she was sorry but Judge Klinkhammer had sentenced them to six months to the same Group Home that I was in. It made me very sad because they weren't bad teenagers, and especially what Mr. Pearson did to me.

When I asked how long I had been in the hospital Mrs. Kowalchuk replied that I had been in a coma and suffering from shock for a week. I remained in the hospital for another two weeks and enjoyed the company of the nurses and sleeping on a real bed. The hospital food was good although other patients called it hash.

Before I was released, a psychologist came to me and some of the questions he asked made me laugh.

The questions were a simple *yes* or *no* format and some of them were: Do I have diarrhea once a month? Is my sex life satisfactory? Do I believe women should have as much freedom as men? Do I prefer the color black to white?

Can a minister cure a disease by praying and putting his hands on one's head? Do ravens steal golf balls in Yellowknife? Is everything in the world turning out as the prophets in the Bible said it would? Are all women psychologists and psychiatrists ugly?

There were one-hundred questions in the test and whatever the psychologist made out of the answers I gave, I don't know. I do know

however, that I wanted to return to the Kent home and Mrs. List said, "No chance."
Mrs. List and I talked for fifteen minutes when she brought me to the Group Home and at the time said, "Don't be sad Sobo because you will have company – the Kowalchuk twins, Joe and Moe, will soon be here."
I could speak no longer because….."

That's where the notebook writing ended with a postscript, "God please grant me the serenity and accept things which I cannot change. Give me the courage the things which I can and the wisdom to know the difference." Underneath those words was a sketch of a dove flying blindly into a crucifix and killing itself.

# CHAPTER TWENTY-FOUR

When Pawel heard about Sobo's suicide he said to himself, "Unfortunately children sometimes don't cry loud enough. How about Joe and Moe? Could the same thing happen to them?"

Pawel also wondered when Sobo would be buried and found when discussions for a funeral took place and Captain Reginald Stone of the Salvation Army said, "When someone dies of suicide the shock and the confusion it causes has severity of its own. Dying by one's hand has different implications that dying of natural causes. The grief that follows is one of the most traumatic in a life."

A funeral service for Sobo was conducted by Captain Stone because it seemed no other church wanted to bury him. Churches weren't tolerant about a person taking his or her own life. Even at St. Anne's Catholic Church Father Ryan said, "Life belongs to God and only He can terminate it."

St. Augustine saw suicide as morally wrong because it was a transgression of the Fifth

Commandment – Thou shall not kill. (Saint's spoke kind of funny in those days).
Father Ryan, when approached about the burial went on, "The church refuses to deal with suicide because it means leaving the victim on consecrated grounds."

Mrs. List, who was appointed to make the burial arrangements, then phoned other churches and found norms prohibiting suicide burials had equally strong in Protestantism, Judaism and Islam. Only the Oriental religions appeared more tolerant on the subject.
At the service Captain Stone said to those who had gathered that some of questions parents, relatives and friends asked themselves in situations like this were: "Why didn't he/she tell us?" "What did I do wrong?" and, "How could the victim do that to me?"
Captain Stone also gave examples of victims leaving notes like Sobo Birch did. A man going blind wrote, "I tried but couldn't continue living in darkness."
And most notes offered an explanation. For instance, a note left by a physician for his

wife merely read, "Forgive me.  It's better this way. No more problems for you. Love."

Near the end of the service Captain Stone said, "Churches must teach compassion towards those who take their own lives. No matter how tragic the mistake, no one has the right to condemn these individuals.  More importantly judgment should be left to God." After a chorus of *Hallelujah's* Captain Stone continued," Time and time again He accepted and pardoned people.  He didn't approve of their sins but He forgave them and loved the sinner. His last words from the cross were words of forgiveness: "Father, forgive them for they do not know what they are doing."

When Captain Stone concluded the service, the casket was brought to a waiting hearse and then to a cemetery overlooking Okanagan Lake where Sobo was buried.
There were no verbal goodbyes and no one except Mrs. Kent to say they were sorry. Following the burial Tina Kent asked Mrs. List to trace the genealogical history of Sobo Birch and was surprised when she revealed,

"Sobo was born out of wedlock and then given up for adoption by Kwitka Kowalchuk.

# CHAPTER TWENTY-FIVE

Funeral services for Sobo ended at 4:00 p. m. at 11;00 Pawel was still in his office at Okanagan Realty discussing with Paul White construction progress of the Lakeshore Mancan Inn.

Whether he looked through a microscope or telescope Pawel agreed contractors were working at high speed and there was a huge crane above piles of lumber, brick and iron rods surrounded by a protective wire fence. White was delighted too how rapidly the building was going up and up and that Pawel going to manage once it was completed.

Minutes later, White left the office and Pawel was going to call it a day too, when the telephone rang. It was Moe at the other end complaining about the Group Home he and Joe were living at.

"Dad," Joe began.

"Speaking."

"Moe and I hate the Group Home and have escaped."

"You what?"

"We escaped."

Pawel wanted to know why.

"The group home father, Mr. Pearson, has been charged with sexually assaulting Sobo Birch, that's why."

"Hurry, Dad. We are already at the Plaza Mall calling from a pay phone next to the Super Value store. Can you please us pick up?"

"I'm on way but remember what probation officer Watson said."

"What?"

"If I assist you in any way I may be charged with contempt of court."

"What do you mean by contempt of court?"

"Good question. It means Judge Klinkhammer may put me into jail. At any rate, stay where you are. I'll be over in ten minutes."

Pawel put out the lights and locked the door. He then hopped into his car and started the motor. The gas gauge registered almost 'Empty' so he drove to the nearest Esso station and filled the gas tank which time to fill it, seemed incredibly long. After paying the account with his credit card, Pawel headed towards the Plaza Mall where Joe and Moe said they would wait.

But when he arrived near the telephone booth no one was there but unusual marks of burned up tire tracks. Instantly Pawel thought Joe and Moe were in difficulty.

"Perhaps they were kidnapped?" he thought wondering what to do next.


Disappointed, Pawel drove back to his apartment recalling various newspaper articles he had read earlier in the week and headlined: *Number of Unsolved Crimes Increases. Killers in California Escaped to Canada* and *Killers Who Kill For the Joy Of Killing.* "What madness is this? It's almost like a state of war. I never have peace with my sons anymore." Pawel said to himself, "We are unsafe on the street, Women get raped, and teenagers are committing suicide. Someone is either protesting or marching about one thing or another. Gracious me, what is this world coming to?"

As Pawel was debating with himself the state of the world, the telephone in his apartment rang. Picking up the receiver after the first ring he said, "Hello."

"Mr. Kowalchuk?"

It was an unfamiliar voice.

"This is Crash London. I use to live in the house on Norton Street that Oknagan Realty has listed for sale."

"Crash who?"

"London."

Pawel initially thought "Crash" was a prospect interested in leasing space at the Lakeshore Mancan Inn once it was completed but that wasn't the case, he was a former tenant who lived in the Norton street dilapidated home.

"So how can I help you?" Pawel asked.

"My partner and I have your sons Joe and Moe. Don't call the police. You can have them back for a ransom of one-million dollars."

"One million!" Pawel exclaimed. "Who do you think I am, the Bank of Canada?"

"Don't get smart, Mr. Kowalchuk. We know your co-partner in the Lakeshore Mancan project is worth a bundle of money."

"So?"

"So you have an important decision to make. It's the money by 4:00 a. m. or else its caput to your sons. They will be digging their own graves."

"Please, there are no banks open until ten," Pawel said when he was interrupted, "It's 4:00 a. m. that you better have the money." There was a clique sound followed by a dial tone.

Precisely at four the phone rang again. It was Crash London with an ultimatum.

Pawel's response was, "I'm sorry but I can't raise one-million in that short time. How about $500,000?"

"Then consider Joe and Moe dead," Crash London said and hung up the phone. Hearing the 'clique' Pawel repeated, "Hello, hello" but to no avail, the line was dead. Feeling uneasy, Pawel slowly walked into the bedroom closet where he picked up a .22 antique rifle that years ago was used by his father to shoot birds and animals for food. The gun gave him a sense of security. With the weapon placed within easy reach he drove and surveyed Penticton's nocturnal life covering all locations where he thought the boys could be hidden

As he was driving he finally said, "Aha, the cemetery where Sobo Birch was buried could be the ideal place"

Pawel approached the cemetery with the headlights turned off to a distance where he noticed four shadows. As he came closer the shadows became distinct people. A deserted graveyard during a dark early raining morning sent chills down Pawel's spine. What he saw next made him horrified. Crash London kept his word and was stabbing Joe and Moe in the back with a butcher knife forcing the boys to dig their own graves with shovels. Boomer Grimes stood by supervising the digging.
"Heaven above, what have we got here?" Pawel said to himself and to London, "Don't move or else I'll shoot."
The attackers did not heed the warning and started running. Pawel pulled the trigger but nothing happened.
He pulled it a second time, and a third; finally realizing the trigger was broken. Pawel was delighted however, that the attackers had fled, no shots were fired and he rescued his sons.
"We want to live with you, Dad," Moe said after he took a deep breath.

"Thank you for rescuing us," Joe continued. Then Pawel had a plan. All he had to do was to execute it. "How would you take to complete your schooling at the Silesian High School in San Francisco?"

"An excellent idea," Joe said.

"But for the plan to work your names should be changed."

"Why? We like our present names."

"So that no one can identify both of you. As it is Sergeant Brown and Mrs. List may be searching for you already."

"What surname do you suggest?" Moe asked, "Instead of Kowalchuk from now onward you will be a Kowal."

"Fine," Joe said and suggested that the name be even shorter. "Instead Kowal let it simply be Ko?"

"And our first names changed to Spider and Rider. I'll be Spider," Moe suggested.

"An excellent Idea," Pawel said, "From now on you are Spider and Rider Ko should anyone ask for identification."

It was understood that if anyone asked Joe or Moe "And what's your name?"

They would say "Spider or Rider Ko."

After everyone got their breath back, "Okay," Pawel said clasping Joe in one arm and Moe in the other. Ten minutes later, they were at Pawel's apartment where each had a shower. Once bloodstains were removed and a hearty breakfast, they traveled south towards the town of Osoyoos and the American/Canadian border where at the American Customs and Immigration office a barrier met them. An officer stepped outside and politely said, "Good morning. Your destination please."

"San Francisco," Pawel answered.

"Anything to declare?"

"No sir."

"And how long are you planning to stay in San Francisco."

"A week."

"You may proceed", the officer said and whished Pawel and the boys an enjoyable journey.

Halfway to Seattle, while Spider and Rider were having a nap, Pawel turned on the radio and on station KING an announcer read a news capsule which included an item about would-be assassins in Penticton who at one time had lived in California and kidnapped Joe and Moe Kowalchuck.

When the announcer completed the newscast he played a Kwitka record and said that the Canadian superstar was presently performing at the Arc Angel nightclub in San Francisco with a date schedule for Seattle the following month.

Pawel drove most of the day before reaching Seattle's International Airport where he registered into a nearby motel, purchased new clothing for Spider and Rider and the threesome spent balance of the evening watching jets landing and taking off at the airport.

# CHAPTER TWENTY-SIX

It wasn`t yet six in the morning, Pawel and his two sons enjoyed a breakfast, parked the car at the Seattle Airport parkade, boarded a jet which when it reached the outskirts of San Francisco and the pilot said, "Prepare for landing. What you see below is the Golden Gate Bridge."

As soon as the jet had landed, Pawel found a telephone directory, the address of the Silesian School for boys and hailed a taxi. When they arrived at the school, a sign greeted them *The Silesians of Don Bosco*. Under the words was a logo, a priest standing in front of a globe with outstretched arms protecting five boys.

As Pawel, Spider and Rider stepped inside the school, Pawel walked up to the receptionist and said, "May I speak with the principal, please?"

"May I tell Father Mark who is it that wishes to see him?"

Pawel was going to say Joe and Moe Kowalchuk but within a second changed his mind and said, "Spider and Rider Ko. Like Kokomo, Indiana."

"Please be seated Father Mark will be right with you."

Within the next minute Father Mark greeted the unexpected visitors, "Good morning, How can I help you?" he said.

"Good morning Father`` Pawel said and went on, "I wonder if we can have a conversation about enrolling Spider and Rider at your school for the remainder of the term?"

The date was March 1957.

"Certainly, let's step into my office that is down the hallway."

When they reached the office Father Mark, six-foot two, dark complexion and sporting a beard said, "Spider and Rider, you must be twins?

The boys said they were.

"Now tell me something about yourselves. First are you Catholic?"

Pawel said they were and gave a brief biographical sketch of himself and the twins.

"And In Penticton what grade are you in school?"

The boys simultaneously said, "Grade eleven."

Father Mark then outlines the school's philosophy and said that the school's first goal was personal growth of the students. That they learn, live and work with others, learn to be responsible and become open to God."

"How about scholastic achievement?" Pawel queried.

"Scholastic achievement must fit with the context. Thus when recording the students' progress, teachers will make notes of their w work, habits and effort."

After still more conversation, Father Mark turned to Pawel and asked, "And to what address shall we mail the report cards?"

On a piece of paper Pawel handed in the address and phone number in the event of an emergency.

After Father Mark discussed the boys' progress or lack of it, he asked Spider, "Do you enjoy sports?"

"Oh, yah, we enjoy boxing most of all.

"Wonderful," Father Mark said, "I enjoy boxing too

We have an excellent program at our school.

And if you decide to take the program, who knows, you may become as good as Sugar Ray Robinson."

After Spider and Rider agreed to take the training, Father asked about their weight. "We are both less than one –hundred and twelve pounds," Rider said which meant they were in the featherweight division.

A short time later, Father Mark brought the boys to their dorm rooms, which weren't fancy but comfortable. Later still, he invited Pawel and his two sons to the cafeteria where they met other students and teachers. As they were enjoying their lunch, they also enjoyed the panoramic view of San Francisco.

"Have you ever been to San Francisco?" Father Mark asked.

"We haven't but intend to as our aunt Kwitka is performing at the Arc Angel."

Father Mark said that he enjoyed Kwitka's music too and went on, "The best way to see San Francisco is from Twin Peaks."

And then gave highlights of several districts including: Telegraph Hill, Knob Hill, and Chinatown, North Beach, Fisherman's wharf and the Haight district.

Father then talked about the city's tradition of non-conformity, its eccentrics, easygoing style, homosexuals, morality and cults.

Near the end of the conversation Rider asked, "San Francisco is made up many people from across the continent?"

"One can say that. They come like pilgrims looking for the Promised Land."

"I guess that is why father is enrolling us at your school," Rider said with a smile.

Father Mark smiled too, "Our school will have you in shape by the time you'll participate in the Golden Glove Boxing Tournament scheduled for Penticton next October."

Pawel and the boys were surprised when Father Mark mentioned *Penticton*.


Upon further conversation he learned that Father Mark was associated with the Silesian School for boys in Edmonton for three years before being transferred to San Francisco. What Father Mark still didn't know however, was that Spider and rider Ko's real name were Joe and Moe Kowalchuk. At this pint Pawel was stricken with guilt because he wasn't truthful so he said, "Father I have a confession to make."

'We do not take confessions until seven o'clock. Can you wait until then?"

"Not that kind of a confession."

"What is it that you want to tell me then?"

"The truth."

"The truth that you do not like our school?"

Pawel shook his head. "The truth is..." but he couldn't complete the sentence so he instead asked, "Father, can you keep a secret?"

"I can."

"The boys."

"What about them?"

Well, their real names are Joe and Moe and the surname is Kowalchuk and not Ko as we introduced ourselves."

Pawel then gave the circumstances of the pseudonyms.

"Under the circumstances I probably would have done the same, "Father Mark said and Pawel continued, "It's imperative that the names remain anonymous until the Lakeshore Mancan Inn in Penticton is completed and the boxing tournament is held."

"We'll leave it to God about the anonymity part but I can tell you that I'm looking forward to next October when I'll be in

Penticton at ringside coaching Spider and Rider, pardon me, Joe and Moe.'

Father Mark paused for several seconds and then said, "I want to know something, Mr. Kowalchuk.'

"What?"

"The bishop has assigned me to do a study on racial prejudice and if you grant me permission to make Spider and Rider look like Black boys when they are in Penticton for the boxing tournament."

"You'll make the boys look like Sugar Ray Robinson."

"Exactly. I'll disguise them with the use of makeup."

"And why do you need makeup?"

"To see if our research bears out that Black People in Canada are discriminated the same way they are in America."

"We'll cooperate."


Prior to leaving the Silesian School for Boys, Pawel, Spider and Rider had an opportunity to spend the afternoon with Kwitka who at night was performing at the Arc Angel nightclub owned by Abe and Raphael Goldman.

When they returned to the school, Pawel discussed with his sons a trip to Italy, which the school had scheduled during the summer holidays.

"I'm delighted you decided to go," Pawel said and went on. "This way you won't have to be back in Penticton until October when the tournament will take place. Further in the conversation he said, "And remember when you do come, you'll look like young men from Africa."

"No problem." Spider said.

What Rider said was, "That will not only surprise Mom but also all of Penticton."

Spider and Rider agreed to go on vacation with a group of boys from the school during the months of July and August.

Upon their return in San Francisco, Father Mark would put on his boxing gloves and sharpen their boxing skills. In the meantime the boys wished their father luck in winning the listing and sales contest that was underway at Okanagan Realty.

"Should you win, will we see you again?" Moe asked.

"I'll do my best not to disappoint you," Pawel replied and that night while Spider and Rider were in the custody of Father Mark and other teachers at the Silesian School For Boys, Pawel took a flight to Seattle where he climbed into his car and drove northward towards Canada.

When Pawel returned to Penticton he thought his worries were over. His first priority was to check on the construction of the Lakeshore Mancan Inn and when he was discussing the project with the foreman the telephone rang. He picked up the receiver after the fourth ring. "Mr. Kowalchuk, please," a familiar voice on the other end said.

"Speaking."

"This is Sergeant Brown with the Penticton police."

"Yes, sergeant, is something the matter?"

"I'm sorry to say but there is."

"What is it?'

"You've been out of town?"

"I have, just returned."

"Then you missed the news about your sons."

"What news?"

"Joe and Moe appear to have been kidnapped from the Group Home and there's no trace of the kidnappers."

"Please tell me more and how much was the ransom?"

"I don't know about the size of ransom but we do know that the kidnappers were identified as Crash London and his accomplice Boomer Grisom."

To assist you with the search did you contact a psychic?"

"And had pictures of Joe and Moe flashed on local television and posted on billboards, at the bus depot and the post office."

"There's a saying that Mounties always get their man," Pawel said. "Now is an opportunity to prove it. By the way, did you notify their mother?"

"We have."

'And?"

"She's quite concerned after we told her that the culprits had escaped from a penitentiary in California and could be serial killers."

Now that construction of the Lakeshore Mancan Inn was nearly completed Paul White decided to retire in Penticton and called on his wife, Erin, to assist him in finding a retirement home.

"The climate in Penticton is more temperate than in Winnipeg," White said to Pawel who took the couple to view homes with lakefronts and acreages. But the home the White's found most attractive was the one occupied by Judge Klinkhammer. The 4800 square foot home was on a one-acre lot, had a panoramic view of Okanagan and Skaha lakes and situated on Ridgedale Avenue.

On the day that an offer on Judge Klinkhammer's home was accepted, Gloria was arranging furniture in her new condominium of Naramata Road. After noticing that kitchen sink faucet was continually running she called on Pawel to see if he could repair it.

Pawel was not a handyman but always wanted his clients to be satisfied, so he arrived at Gloria's condo with a set of pliers and a wrench. After the faucet was repaired, Pawel casually said, "Gloria, it would give me great pleasure if you joined me for dinner.

"I was hoping you would ask," Gloria said and that evening they hopped into Pawel's car, drove to Granny Bognar's Restaurant where at a secluded corner table they discussed a number of things important to their lives and said, "Gloria you are fantastic, I'm still turned on by you today, as much as I was on our first date."

Then during the following week Gloria went to local radio media recounting her wrong doing and mistakes and to a reporter said, "I'm happy for Pawel that the Lakeshore Mancan Inn will be officially opened soon." The reporter in turn said, "Why do you feel that way?"

"Because, I was foolish to oppose its construction in the first place. I realize it was a mistake and I was harsh on him. I'll ask for pardon. Will he accept my apology, who knows?"

Next day, while Pawel and Gloria met for a lunch she confirmed the possibility, "I certainly will and one thing more."

"What, dear?" Pawel said.

"I want to reconcile and be by your side during the ribbon cutting ceremony."

"That would make me happy."

Then Gloria said, "We've been separated for a year. Why would you want me back?"

"Because, what's the use of having an Inn if there's no one to share it with. I always wanted something more for the children and you, than for myself."

"Good point. You have no idea how uncomfortable it's been living without you."

"I don't know what to say except that one can't resolve problems by condemning it. And do you want to know something else?"

"What?" Pawel said,

"I still love you."

"And I love you too. I'm certain we can make it work if we accept each other for what we are. To tell you the truth I found the idea of a legal separation repulsive."

"So did I. Do you know what day this is?"

"The happiest day of my life."

"And our twentieth wedding anniversary."

"How can I forget, how can I deny, that all this time you were the love of my life."

Gloria was drawn to Pawel and him for his part, willing to accept her as his wife again despite being separated for a year.

And then Gloria asked about Joe and Moe.

"Can you keep a secret?" Pawel said.

"I can. I swear not to tell anyone."

"Well, Joe and Moe have not been kidnapped as many are led to believe. At this very moment they are touring Italy with Father Mark and a group of boys from the Silesian School for Boys in San Francisco. The boys are also training for a boxing tournament, which will be held in Penticton during the upcoming Wine festival."

Pawel then went on to tell Gloria that Joe and Moe were using the fictitious names of Spider and Rider Ko.

"And in addition to that, the boys will be made to appear like Black boys from Africa.

"Why on earth for?"

"Because their teacher and trainer, Father Mark, is conducting a research project to determine if Canadian Afro boxers are prejudiced against like they are in America."

The reconciliation took place at a time when all of Penticton was looking forward to the official opening of the Lakeshore Mancan Inn at which time the Canadian Real Estate Association of Canada was about to hold a convention. The hotel was also booked for the Wine Festival and a National boxing tournament scheduled to follow.

# CHAPTER TWENTY-SEVEN

Within hours the Lakeshore Mancan Inn was about to be officially opened while a convention of the Canadian Real Estate Association had already begun. Kwitka was waiting in her room to perform in the evening as part of the opening celebration.

Canadian Real Estate Association activities already began with the annual golf tournament and the Sunday evening a whoop-up night that included a fun-filled evening featuring games of chance, free beer and hotdogs.

Monday was launched with a breakfast and officially the real estate convention started at 9:00 a. m. American's most exciting inspirational team, Bob and Rita Million, from New York City, were keynote speakers. Their topic was, "How to Be a Super Star in Real Estate."

All business sessions featured a panel of experts and a moderator who handled the predetermined questions about residential, farm and ranch, commercial and management properties.

In addition questions were asked from the floor and the subject of *Security* came up often. Penticton's beautiful setting and moderate climate was virtually a guarantee to a relaxing and an enjoyable convention.

When evening arrived, it was time for the Lakeshore Mancan Inn official opening ceremonies and three-thousand people gathered on the front lawn to witness the historic occasion. Another group of one-hundred invited guests sat in an area bedecked with flowers and plants at the front entrance of the twelve-story building where British Columbia's Minister of Tourism handed Pawel and Paul White a large pair of scissors so they could cut the red ribbon.

In his speech the Minister took a moment to compliment Pawel and Paul White as co-venture.

"The Lakeshore Mancan Inn is one of the most striking buildings in all of British Columbia," the minister said and went on,

"The skyline, the landscaping, the surroundings and all the amenities that blend into a perfect setting which I'm certain will attract multi-national companies to hold their conventions in Penticton."

The Minister went on to say that because of the 'Inn' other hotels and motels were steadily improving the occupancy.

"There already has been a modest improvement which has allowed hotels and motels to operate at a break-even point."

Next, the Minister approached Pawel and White and as they cut the ribbon together, the Minister said, "We now declare the Penticton Mancan Inn officially opened."

Those on the front lawn exploded with a thunderous applause. Downtown businesses reacted favorably when Mayor Edwards walked up to the microphone and for his part said, "We should all say 'Thank you' Pawel Kowalchuck and Paul White for such a magnificent building and having faith in the Peach City as the leading fun centre in British Columbia."

Following the complement the Mayor went on, "This is an example of free enterprise in action with the environment in mind."

There were other speakers too. For his part the general contractor said, "My men worked feverishly to meet a deadline. I'm proud of the Penticton Mancan Inn, it's the finest building our company has ever built."

There were speeches by the local member of the legislature, the Member of Parliament and the president of the Chamber of Commerce who spoke of the potential business and spin-offs the hotel would draw from outside the province.

As soon as the congratulatory speeches were done, a piper marched in and played a Scottish tune. He was followed by Captain Stone of the Salvation Army who in his dedication said, "I dedicate this hotel, Lakeshore Mancan Inn, in the name of God."

As soon as the opening ceremonies were over, Pawel and Paul White invited those present to tour the facilities while the realtors' in turn were about to take part in the Real Estate ball whose theme was a period of British Columbia history – Mounties, mining and whiskey.

It was turning out to be a most enjoyable evening and excitement permeated throughout the hotel. The real estate ball was the first official formal function since the Mancan Inn was built and champagne corks never seemed to cease popping. Soon musicians began playing and Pawel and Gloria were the first couple on the dance floor. They were followed by Paul and Erin White, and then the real estate delegates and their wives. When the appropriate time came Kwitka came on stage and sang popular hits of the day including the hit *I Apologize,* which she had just recorded in her album.

While the band and Kwitka took a midnight break, Don Ferguson, owner and agent of Okanagan Realty, and master of ceremonies, took the microphone at centre stage and announced a scavenger hunt.

"Ladies and gentlemen, a scavenger hunt is about to begin and last one hour, he began and then outlined the rules. First prize was a case of Pride of the Okanagan—Vintage 1957 wine vinted by Roman and Evdokia Kowalchuk.

After naming the prizes Ferguson said, "I want everyone back in the ballroom with a bottle of whiskey at least ten years old, a lump of genuine British Columbia coal and a live policeman in uniform."

As the band and Kwitka were enjoying their break most of the couples formed into groups of four and slipped away to find article they needed to bring back.
Pawel and Gloria teamed up with Paul and Erin White and headed straight for the White residence on Ridgedale. On the way Pawel said, "No problem we can easily find a policeman in uniform even it means getting Sergeant Brown out of bed."
"And how about the whiskey?" Gloria asked.
"We have some at our residence," Erin replied. "But a lump of coal?  That's going to be a problem."
"I'll phone my secretary. She's knowledgeable on matters like coal," Pawel said. "That may be difficult because Penticton uses oil and natural gas as fuel," Paul White said.

When the two couples arrived at the White residence Pawel phoned his secretary at her residence to solicit help in finding a lump of coal.

"I'll call right back as soon as I find some," the secretary said. "What's your telephone number?"

Pawl gave it to her.

As soon as the secretary hung up Paul White said, "Look, Pawel, a host to a convention shouldn't win a prize. It would be more appropriate if someone from out of town had the honor of winning the scavenger hunt."

"An excellent idea. What you say makes sense. It would appear as if it was a fix if we won a case of my parents' wine as a prize. Instead let's relax and return to the Lakeshore Mancan Inn party in an hour."

While Pawel and Paul White were enjoying each other's company in the living room, Erin and Gloria went to the kitchen to make coffee.

"What a good day this has been," Pawel said to White. "The opening ceremonies went off without a glitch. And Penticton may not be heaven but it's the next best thing."

As soon as Pawel said those words two thugs appeared from the bedroom and the taller said, "Don't move. Do as you are told."

And the shorter one said, "Perfect, Mr. Kowalchuk and Mr. White at the same time. Stay calm or else both of you will be dead." The taller while pointing a gun at White said, "We demand a million dollars and a flight to Iran. Your deadline is 8:00 a. m. our time. It was 12:30 a. m in Penticton.

Pawel recognized the two men as Crash London and his accomplice Boomer Grimes. "You won't get away with this like you did when you kidnapped my sons Joe and Moe," Pawel said.

"Shut up!" London screamed.

White was stalling for time. "A million dollars I haven't got at the moment, how about fifty-thousand?"

London looked towards Grimes whose knife was near Pawel's throat. Grimes nodded his head signifying approval.

"Okay, for a start we'll take the fifty-thousand London said and followed White to a bedroom where the money was kept in a safe. Minutes later London and White returned to the living room where Pawel continued,

"Now that you have the fifty-thousand, leave us alone before police arrive."

"Not before we talk to Mrs. White," London replied and while Grimes guarded White and Pawel, he walked quietly into the kitchen where Erin and Gloria were chatting and the telephone rang.

"Answer it!" London said startling the two women and at the same time pointing a gun at Erin. "And don't do anything funny!"

Erin picked up the receiver after the fourth ring. On the other end was Pawel's secretary who said she had found lumps of coal for the scavenger hunt.

"I'll give him the message,"

"Can I speak to Pawel?"

"Sorry but he's not available."

By the way Erin was speaking the secretary felt something was wrong. After a brief one-sided conversation the secretary said, "Simply answer yes or no. Is something the matter?"

"Yes," Erin said and hung up the receiver.

On the other end of the line, after hearing a dial tone, the secretary said to herself, "Something definitely is the matter at the White residence.

Better call the police," and when she did, she said to the civilian guard, "Quick, there's something the matter at the White residence on Rdgedale Avenue."

She gave the address and phone number. Hearing the concern the civilian guard replied, "There's no policeman available at the moment. It seems there's a real estate convention going on at the Lakeshore Mancan Inn and all policeman on duty have been captured as part of a scavenger hunt."

"What? No police protection! What are we paying taxes for?" the secretary protested. "I insist there's something wrong at the White residence on Ridgedale Avenue that needs immediate attention."

"I'm not suggesting that you are putting me on or that this is a crank phone call," the security guard said, "The point is that no policemen are available at the moment. I'll page the Lakeshore Mancan Inn, however, and see if their security can make contact with Sergeant Brown."

Inside White's tension-filled home Pawel and White were tied up and duct taped but not Erin and Gloria. They were released.

By now Sergeant Brown got the message and was gathering his co-workers for a rescue. Pawel's real estate training became handy as he managed to smooth talk London who obviously was the leader, by suggesting counter offers.

"If you leave us alone you can work in the hotel as a security guard."

"And your friend in the house keeping department," White went on.

Later, White tried to make the captors realize that getting money at nighttime from a Winnipeg bank was a lengthy and a complicated process.

"But it's already dawn in Winnipeg," London said. "The banks will open soon."

"Not quite," White said. "In Winnipeg it's only 5:00 a. m."

It was 2:00 a. m. in Penticton.

London turned on the television as an alert television crew was already describing the hostage taking. Then a reporter on the *News Hour* intoned, "American authorities have confirmed that Crash London was responsible for twelve murders in San Francisco and

Canada. It's believed his last victims were Joe and Moe Kowalchuk in Penticton."
London and Grimes seemed nervous but waited for the Winnipeg banks to open. Sergeant Brown and Penticton police meanwhile were getting organized and the media gathered.

After Erin and Gloria returned to the hotel, where they were placed under special security, the RCMP tactical team arrived armed with high velocity rifles equipped with periscope mirrors for seeing around corners. Brown instructed six of these men to take positions close to the White home behind trees, shrubs and walls. He also made arrangements with a neighbor to use the telephone and had Erin draw a sketch of her home's floor plan for police.
Onlookers, many realtors from the convention, brought lawn chairs and radios while the press ranks swelled too.
"It's better than the movies and it's free," one reporter said to another while waiting patiently.

By 4:00 a. m. police, now numbering the full city compliment of 34 men and some from neighboring municipalities, set up a telephone hookup. The Staff Sergeant was now ready for action and to talk to Crash London.

The drama had spread not only throughout Penticton but throughout rest of Canada when on the next bulletin the television announcer said, "There's a standoff in Penticton."

Inside, Pawel Kowalski and Paul White had been taken into the master bedroom presumably to give London a better view of the tack team he had been told about on TV and radio bulletins.

Then came the first of many phone calls. London answered all of them and reminded Brown on the other end of the line about his demands. "You have just one hour left. A million dollars and a safe flight to Cuba. If the money isn't here by then, its goodbye Paul White and Pawel Kowalchuk."

For the next while, London and Grimes seemed reasonable and rational when White said to both that the banks were still closed.

It was just a matter of hours and phone calls, and then ransom money would be on its way. As soon the deadline arrived, London knew it was 1O:00 a. m. in Winnipeg, but White convinced him to extend the deadline another hour so the funds could be transferred from Winnipeg to Penticton.

In another phone call Sergeant Brown confirmed what White had said, "It takes time. A million dollars isn't that easy to transfer and furthermore it takes time to arrange an aircraft to fly you direct to Iran." What wasn't said was that no one had been in touch with a bank in Winnipeg and various plans among the police to capture London and Grimes.

"Dead or alive, it doesn't matter", Brown instructed his men.

In a later call, Brown said to London, "We now have your million dollars and an aircraft is waiting at the Penticton Airport. The car delivering the money will be here shortly." While Brown and London were on the telephone, in what seemed like a drawn out conversation, four tactical squad members had sneaked into the downstairs of the house through an unlocked back door.

Two crawled to a position in the kitchen and the other two hid in an adjoining room. The stairs from the bedroom descended into the hallway that was connected to the two rooms. The four police snipers waited.

In another call to Crash London Sergeant Brown told the increasingly nervous London, "The money will be left inside the kitchen door and a car will be waiting to drive you to the airport."

Outside, reporters observed an unmarked police car drive along Ridgedale Avenue to the White residence to drop the money.

Inside, London asked White, Pawel and Grimes to accompany him down a flight of stairs.

Still bound, the captives shuffled along step by step and London held his .357 magnum next to White's head and Grimes a knife to Pawel's back. Pushing through the swinging door into the kitchen London saw a black suitcase and said to White, "You may pick it up."

From the same room came a voice, "Don't move, police!"

Crash London and Boomer Grimes pulled their captors in front of them and before they could fire a shot or stab anyone the M-16 in policemen's hands rang out. Police bullets pierced London's heart and Grime's head, splattering blood on the empty packsack.

White and Pawel fell to the floor too but their injuries weren't serious. Soon sirens screamed outside as two ambulances arrived and attendants loaded London and Grimes into one and White and Pawel into another.
"Police did a splendid job," White said to Pawel as the ambulance driver took them to the Penticton Regional Hospital.
"They certainly did," Pawel agreed,
The press and spectators finally unfettered, charged up Ridgedale Avenue as soon as they learned that the main characters had just whizzed by then and that London and Grimes were dead. The only excitement spectators enjoyed was the sound of two gunshots. When the drama was over, those present either went home, back to work, the Lakeshore Mancan Inn or break news of Crash London and Boomer Grimes to the world.

Dr. Singh at the hospital, after examining Pawel and White, said, "Neither Mr. White or Mr. Kowalchuk was seriously injured but they will spend rest of the day at the hospital for observation and a deserved rest."

The following day before Pawel and White were dismissed, Sergeant Brown called a news conference in the hospital boardroom. Brown confirmed the London and Grimes had lived in Norton street house for eleven months before disappearing.

"In addition to that," Brown continued. "American authorities have confirmed that London murdered at least a dozen people in greater San Francisco."

Then White interjected," Policemen saved our lives."

"Pawel went on, "There were times during the hostage crises I had doubts if we were going to make it through."

Before Pawel and White knew what was what, they faced media reporters with a barrage of questions one of which was, "What do you think led to the hostage taking?"

"Greed," Brown replied.

Another question followed, "Did you ever think that because of the scavenger hunt Penticton was left without police protection? And how about Joe and Moe?"

Some reporters abandoned their own questions and picked up on the last one. When everyone quieted down for an answer, Pawel replied, "I would rather not comment about Joe and Moe at this time."

For some reason the comment caused a sensation. Memos were scribbled; reporters ran for the nearest telephone and returned. Flashbulbs popped and a TV camera focused on Pawel for a close-up. Pawel began to sweat fearing the news had been leaked out somehow that Joe and Moe were attending the Silesian School for Boys in San Francisco.

"Now another question," another reporter said, "Is it true that you and Gloria have reconciled your differences and are living together again?"

"The answer your questions are *yes*, in both areas."

Pawel also knew the reply *yes* would lead to further questions so he politely said, "Members of the press, let's limit the questions to what happened at the White residence on Ridgedale Avenue."

All Pawel now wished was to conclude the news conference as quickly as possible. His last comment led reporters to ask Sergeant Brown, "What took you so long to apprehend London and his accomplice?" to which he replied, "Our office had been compiling a day to day grid of London's movements. We nearly caught him last night but a realtor attending the convention and participating in the scavenger hunt, flagged me down. Thinking it was something urgent I stopped the patrol car but the realtor grabbed me by the arm and said I was needed at the Lakeshore Mancan Inn. Being a good sport and thinking it was a charitable work, I discovered later, I was part of the scavenger hunt."

"I hear London was an international criminal," another reporter asked.

"That's true. His exploits have made him a macabre hero in California, mostly murdering wealthy people and their sons and daughters.

Some killings included repeated stabbings with a knife, others strangulations by hand and in some cases with a garrote. I wouldn't be surprised if Joe and Moe Kowalchuk are included in his list of victims."

Pawel remained silent.

As the press conference was concluding, a reporter more intrepid than the rest, asked Pawel, "What's next?"

Pawel responded with, "The Penticton Wine Festival and the Golden Glove Boxing Tournament that will soon take place on the same day."

# CHAPTER TWENTY-EIGHT

Wine lovers from throughout the Okanagan Valley gathered in Penticton for the October 1957 Wine Festival, which usually took place during the last week of September and the first of October. To coincide with the festival the Golden Glove Boxing Tournament was also scheduled.

For several years now the festival was a big weekend for visitors and local folk alike. For $10.00 the participants could sample wine from Penticton grown grapes. The year 1957 was no exception and vintners reported an excellent crop although some complained their profit was smaller than usual because of unusual storms.

First thing on Saturday morning, impartial wine tasters from Bulgaria, France and California toured the Purple Grape Vineyard and enjoyed the fruits of Roman and Evdokia's labor. Roman acted as tour director and host as the four men walked through the vineyard and workers were still picking up the last grapes on slopes, some so steep, they would dizzy the average mountain goat. All work was done by hand, men and women, and some of the workers were on their knees trimming the last vines and dreaming of their pay cheques.

Roman said to the wine tasters as they walked along, "No wonder good wine costs so much. First we had the storms damage the vines and then were two weeks behind but the weather since has improved. Early frost would have been a disaster."

The picturesque Okanagan Valley with its homes on crests of hills, manicured gardens near the chain of lakes, vineyards and orchards, made a perfect scene.

"Beautiful and peaceful like in France but there's something missing the French taster said about the surroundings.

"And what is that?" Roman asked.

"There is no sound of church bells from ancient monasteries."

"You are right, no monks, no nuns," the California taster said and then while picking up a handful of the grapes, went on, "But I have never seen such perfect grapes. It seems a shame to crush them."

The wine taster from Bulgaria agreed. "The certainly are nice grapes."
The California taster said the economic downturn had created a poor domestic market in his state, which was why most of company's wines were exported to Canada, Australia and Great Britain.

\As the wine tasters were touring the Purple Grape Vineyard they found a barrel of wine Roman had forgot to close and still open. Beside the barrel were a dozen birds – dead drunk. Roman handled the awkward situation with skill. After closing the barrel the birds sobered up and flew away.
Without saying this was a situation Roman wished it had not happened, but minutes later the tasters hopped into a four-wheel drive and Roman drove them to other vineyards near Highway 97 at Okanagan Falls, Oliver and Osoyoos. It was a cloudy day and prospects for a storm looked good. Along the way there were gardens, vineyards and fruit stands.

Following the vineyard tour the tasters, along with other people, gathered for the parade through downtown Penticton which became a stage for rest of Canada as a major TV network telecast it. From the civic point of view this was a chance for Penticton to gain national publicity – first the parade, the tasting of the wine competition and then the finals of the Golden Glove Boxing Tournament.

Almost everyone dressed in ethnic costumes, including Mayor Edwards and his wife. There were marching bands, decorated cars and floats in a kaleidoscope of colors. There was the *Mr. and Mrs. Wine* float, the *B. C. Fruit* float and floats representing each ethnic group and major industry in the Okanagan Valley. Mayor Edwards headed the parade in a 1911 Rolls Royce. He was followed by Miss Wine 1957, Miss Wine from California was there also, and so were unicycle riders, clowns and various bands: a tuba band, a boy's drum corps, and girls twirling flags, many from the neighboring American states.

As the parade passed the Mayor's float stopped to talk with the TV announcer who was describing the event.

"Penticton invites the world to taste our wine and food," the Mayor said speaking into a camera focused on him. "We are holding a party at the Lakeshore Mancan Inn. This will be followed by boxing matches, which should appeal to future Olympians. The city is saddened however, that two of our prominent teenage boxers, Joe and Moe Kowalchuk, are not with us to participate in the tournament." After the announcer asked what had happened to Joe and Moe, the Mayor answered the best way he could and then went on, "I invite everyone to celebrate Septoberfest with Penticton."

After the Mayor spoke for another minute he added, "Take our Okanagan Valley wine for instance. Because of our moderate climate we are not far behind California. Good wines begin with good grapes. In places like Chile, even New York State, wines are judged on their own merit and not against French wines. Strange as it is we are led to believe that the best of everything come from somewhere

else: Swiss watches, Japanese cars, American technology and French wine, clothing and perfumes. But when it comes to wines, mark my word, Penticton will soon lead the world and provide a dash of character of its own."
The parade came to an end when the last entry, a pipe band from Kelowna, played *Scotland the Brave*. Later, guests that included Kwitka, assembled at the Lakeshore Mancan Inn for the wine tasting competition and dinner which was first rate: quail eggs in potato baskets with a fresh herb sauce, ox tail consommé, roast beef, preserved pears and all the local wines one wanted to drink.

Following the dinner, the three wine tasters walked to a table with all sorts of bottles with labels covered up.
"Gentlemen, three wines," the wine tasting chairman said, "Simple problem, identify the best sweet, medium and dry wine."
The tasting highlighted the way in which local wines, even when using the same grapes, had different styles, aromas and tastes. This year, despite severe storms, the vineyards had tended to produce rich fully ripened grapes with high sugar content and flavor.

Although there were exceptions the wines tended to be full-bodied as well.

The first wines, the tasters decided to go by smell alone. The Bulgarian tasted the first bottle as he swished, swirled, chewed and circled his lips, then spit into an open can. The California and French taters did the same and then an attendant came and took the bottle away.

There were twelve competitive categories for entries and four of these were restricted to wine made from 100% Okanagan Valley grown grapes. These tended to attract the most attention. On the whole the standard of entries marked an advance over competitions held in previous years. Most interesting wines were those entered in the white Vinefera category and according to an enologist of the federal government agriculture research centre in Summerland, the year had a good chance to produce the best *Pride of the Okanagan* wine ever vinted.

He predicted Pride of the Okanagan – vintage 1957, would be the vintage of the half-century, "Even better than Pride of the Okanagan – vintage 1919," he said.

"Three more wines and this time by taste." the tasting chairman said to the tasters. "Look for the hallmark of good Okanagan wine with sweetness and acidity. In your opinion, of all the entries, which is the best wine?"

Again swish, swirl, chew, circle of lips and a spit into an empty can. The ritual was followed by tasters nodding their heads and an attendant taking the bottles away. After fifteen minutes the unmistakable character of the best wine vinted in Penticton that year was announced.

"Ladies and gentlemen," the wine tasting chairman began, "May I please have your attention? The overall winner is Pride of the Okanagan – vintage 1957. The winners are Roman and Evdokia Kowalchuk proprietors of the Purple Grape Vineyard."

There was a gentle applause as the respective winners went to the head table to pick up medals, ribbons and trophies. In accepting his trophy Roman gave a statement on the Purple Grape Vineyard estate winery. He said, "Evdokia and I are deeply honored in accepting this award. You should know however, that in making wine our costs are fixed, our yield isn't.

Our pickers work long hours and last week I bought a bottle of imported wine for a lower price than ours."

Near the end of his acceptance speech, Roman said, "Wine is intimate, full of purpose, romantic but we must educate the public so it can say 'No' to wine with fancy bottles."

As soon as the wine tasting ceremony was over those inside the Lakeshore Mancan Inn spread out into the front side lawn where Pawel and Gloria were amazed at the large number of visitors as they walked and talked along the shore of Okanagan Lake and fed Canada geese, mallard ducks, trumpeter swans and seagulls until they came upon a scene where swinging hips began cajoling the audience from the stage of the amphitheater outside Polynesia.

There was still plenty of daylight as the festival continued. Late on the same stage Spanish dancers clicked castanets and tapped heels. Then the Chinese dancers took the stage and moved gracefully to Oriental music. A short time later, Chief Wandering Spirit, from a nearby reserve joined Indians and together they did a dance for peace.

Later still Kwitka came on stage, sang and danced, and when she was through received a thunderous applause.

Suddenly a sharp gust of wind played havoc with some of the booths set up for the occasion but emergency work was done and the wind and the cloudy sky didn't daunt throngs that had gathered from sampling different wines and food, to applaud entertainers outside, and to experience being on Lakeshore Mancan Inn landscaped grounds.

The food outside, featured samples from throughout the world. German cooks had a flare for dishes using Okanagan Valley fruit. Italians featured spaghetti and meatballs; Poles pierogi and kielbasa, native Indians, banac and mushrooms; Ukrainians, borscht and holubtsi. Even Dr. Singh had a booth displaying food from India.

The aroma of the food drifted across the entire Lakeshore Mancan Inn landscape with sounds of the oompah bands scattered throughout. There was the local pipe band, the high school band conducted by Frank Tarafaski, and there were American bands, all had taken part in the parade and each strategically placed.

Most of the 15,000 people who crowded into the Lakeshore Mancan Inn property were from out of town. They came by buses, cars, campers, and motorbikes and some even hitchhiked.

"People are still coming in large numbers, in droves actually," is how the same TV announcer who described the parade earlier, informed his viewers. The announcer broke into regular programs with bulletins.

"I'm not certain which the main attraction is: the Lakeshore Mancan Inn, the Wine Festival, Kwitka's presence or the Golden Glove Boxing Tournament which is scheduled to follow shortly."

As soon as darkness came, many of those who had gathered for the Wine Festival began drifting back into the Lakeshore Mancan Inn and some into a large room where the Golden Boxing Tournament was about to begin. As Pawel and Gloria were making their entrance Mayor Edwards grabbed Gloria by the hand and said, "See, as soon as you let construction of the building take its course the Lakeshore

Mancan Inn became compatible with the surrounding environment."

Gloria agreed the structure was one of the finest in Canada and the landscaping next to it was most innovative and neither Versailles Gardens in Paris, those in Niagara Falls or the Butchard gardens in Victoria, B. C. could match.

"The well-landscaped grounds and the Lakeshore Mancan Inn are a perfect example how harmony between man and environment can exist," Gloria said.

"It wasn't easy, but I'm proud of the structure, and delighted to be loved again."

Already in the auditorium, with an excellent view of the boxing ring, were Roman and Evdokia. Sitting next to them were Jacques and Yvette Gateau, Chief Dion and his wife Elizabeth; Lee and Sen Wong and Isaiah Alexander and his wife Patty, who traveled from Bonnyville. As this small group of people were chitchatting and exchanging pleasantries, Evdokia said that she wasn't a boxing fan while Roman said he and Evdokia made a wise decision by moving from Bonnyville to Penticton.

"Boxing matches by their very nature aren't pretty things," Paul White said to Pawel. "Noses are broken, eyes are blackened and boxers get hurt."

"All this is true," Pawel replied and went on, "These are the same experiences we went through while building the Lakeshore Mancan Inn and Gloria and I went through in our marriage. But kids want to box and it shows in their competitive spirit one certainly needs to achieve a goal."

As Pawel said those words Spider (Joe) walked into the ring under the pretext of being a black-colored teenager.

"I know very little about boxing," Erin said and then asked, "Why is the crowd booing the kid who is entering the boxing ring?"

Pawel's reply was, "Because people change like the wind. The boy is being booed because those watching him think he's of African heritage."

Only Gloria was told that Spider (Joe) and Rider (Moe) were wearing makeup throughout their body skillfully applied by Father Mark, their trainer.

Paul White continued, "As far as I'm concerned boxing has been associated with city ghettos and regarded as an activity in which young men participate because it's the only way out for them."

What White had said wasn't exactly true because at the Silesian School for Boys in San Francisco, Joe and Moe learned not to complain when they lost and to be gracious whenever they won. When they lost they didn't make excuses or seek scapegoats. They fought as well as they could against opponents who also dreamed of making the Rome Summer Olympics in 1960.

"Everyone knows about dreams," Gloria said as he edged in closer to Pawel.

Pawel agreed, "Nowhere is that dream more common than in the real estate industry."

At that moment the ring announcer intoned, "In the blue corner, weighing 111 pounds and from Vancouver, British Columbia…"

Several seconds later the announcer introduced Spider (Joe Kowalchuk).

"And in the red corner, weighing 108 pounds and from San Francisco, California, is Spider Ko. His trainer is Father Mark.

Those in the audience booed again.

When the first round began the booing subsided because the Caucasian boxer came on strong making Spider look awful. By the time the second round came it was a different story –Spider's left jab, which worked only moderately well in the first round, caught the other boxing napping.

Spider's right hand seemed to come alive and he popped the other boxer with hard rights and looping lefts. Spider's timing, his ability to bob and weave and slip punches had the crowd booing again. The Caucasian boxer was their favorite.

After the bell rang for the third and final round Spider leg go several more hard rights and lefts and the other boxer was bleeding but determined. Halfway through the round Spider let go a right and rocked the other boxer who was forced to take a mandatory eight count.

Thirty seconds Spider kissed his right glove and bid his opponent goodnight. He stunned the other boxer with hard rights knocking him to the canvass. When the other boxer   picked himself up, Spider moved in for the kill.

Twenty seconds later the referee moved in to give the other boxer another 8 count. At 2:23 of the round Spider sent the other boxer back to the canvass with another right and a left hook. The referee then moved in to stop the fight officially.

When it was Rider's turn to enter the ring he was as black colored as Spider was and the audience booed him too.
As the first round was about to begin Father Mark said to Rider, "This is a big fight. Measure your opponent up in the first round. Just do your best.
Use your discretion and don't forget people who are watching. Think you are a Black boxer. Don't let the booing get you down."

For the first two rounds Rider seemed anxious to land his knockout punch, which left him open to some hard blows from his opponent and cheers from the audience. In the third round however, Rider was more cautious, scoring with combinations and counter punches.

The Caucasian opponent was on the receiving end and when the round was near an end, the boxers stood toe-to-toe punching each other. As soon as the bout was over, the judges handed in their scorecard and the ring announcer said, "By unanimous decision, the winner is Rider Ko."

The ring announcer then raised Rider's arms into the air and congratulated him, "Well done."

But the crowd booed again.

Following the tournament tears flowed freely from Pawel and Gloria's eyes after they had seen their sons win two decisions. Under the rules of amateur boxing, where points for a love tap are worth as much as for a severe blow, both parents were proud of Joe and Moe's achievement and their own..

Gloria accompanied Pawel into the dressing room and introduced her to Father Mark. "Thank you for taking care of Joe and Moe," Gloria said while shaking the priest's hand. "Pawel has often spoken about you."

"Well, does your research prove anything?" Pawel asked.

"It does."

"Curious, Pawel said," What?"
"What I feared the most. That there is discrimination against Black people in Canada as there is in America.

Now that the boxing tournament was over Pawel faced a problem – how was he going to return Joe and Moe to San Francisco so they continued with their schooling and at the same time not revealing their true identity."
"First you better call Sergeant Brown," Gloria suggested
Once the policeman arrived and Pawel explained what had happened to Joe and Moe he said to Pawel, "I'm sorry but you are under arrest."
"What for?"
"Contempt of Court."
"By that you meant?"
"You were told not to interfere with Joe's and Moe's sentence to the Group Home."

"It's a good thing he did," Gloria said. "Haven't you heard what happened to Sobo Birch who stayed in the same Group Home?"
"I have," the Staff Sergeant replied and after some soul searching went on, "All right.

Mr. Pearson's action eventually let to Sobo Birch's suicide. It was a terrible tragedy."

The contempt of court charge against Pawel was eventually dropped and proper papers filled out with United States Immigration authorities so Joe and Moe could return to San Francisco and continue with their education. In the process Joe and Moe made peace with their mother and so did Evdokia with Gloria. Now that Pawel realized his boyhood dream of building an Inn on the shore of a beautiful lake, he and Gloria settled their differences and from that day onward lived in a penthouse of the Lakeshore Mancan Inn.

Kwitka continued to entertain throughout the world while Roman and Evdokia vinted some of the finest wine ever tasted. Sitting in the backyard overlooking the vineyard Roman and Evdokia were enjoying a glass of wine as the brilliant sun that evening exploded into shimmering multi-colors and was about to set. It was October 24, 1957, the thirtieth anniversary since Pawel Kowalchuk arrived in Canada.

To mark the occasion, Roman and Evdokia put on their sheepskin vests, which were, stiffened somewhat over the years. Some of the intricate embroidery along the edges was frayed. But the hand woven hemp peasant costumes the Kowalchuk's wore when they arrived exactly thirty years earlier, were still in excellent condition thanks to the loving care given by Roman and Evdokia who were sitting next to each other and she said, "My, oh, my. How things have changed since we arrived in Canada from Ukraine."

Roman agreed, "First we had to fight to survive. Now we survive but fight to maintain decent values."

Evdokia then put her glass of wine to one side and said, "Now I realize how lucky we are to be Canadians."

"Lucky? Why so?"

"Because historians have confirmed, that Stalin has murdered seven-million Ukrainians and we aren't one of them. It's a big puzzle why did Moscow decide to starve them to death? I can think only of few other nations that have suffered as much as Ukraine in its history as a nation."

44268524R00237

Made in the USA
Charleston, SC
21 July 2015